lonely planet

POCKET STOCKHOLM

Nanjala Nyabola

Contents

Top: Dala horses in a Stockholm shop
Bottom: Stortorget (p45)

Explore Stockholm 33

Stockholm Toolkit 143

FROM TOP LEFT: MAURIZIO DE MATTEI/SHUTTERSTOCK ©, KIRK FISHER/SHUTTERSTOCK ©

★ Top Experiences

The Journey Begins Here

Stockholm whispers cool across any era, whether it's the old buildings and museums or restaurants that overflow with stylish clientele regardless of the weather. A network of islands, each with a slightly different character, Stockholm is united by this unspoken commitment to remaining effortlessly elegant and yet also accessible. You won't find many big brash attractions here: most of its charm comes from being able to exist at a chilled pace – in a small, niche museum, nibbling on local fare, enjoying a free festival or indulging in your favourite sport. Cool is not something that you work at. It just is, and that is Stockholm.

Nanjala Nyabola
@nanjalaone
Nanjala loves to travel, climb mountains, run marathons and write about it all. She has researched several cities for Lonely Planet.

Gamla Stan (p35)
MISTERVLAD/SHUTTERSTOCK ©

THE BEST

Museum Experiences

One thing you will not run out of in Stockholm is museums to visit, from grand sweeping historical collections to small, niche affairs. Take your pick!

Enjoy a snapshot of Sweden's extensive history at the **Nationalmuseum**, which also hosts extensive programming for kids. (pictured, p152)

Nerd out at the informative and interactive installations at **Tekniska Museet**. (p110)

Encounter the greats of photography and related arts at the world-renowned **Fotografiska**. (p90)

Wander through the delights of the world's first open-air museum at **Skansen**. (p85)

Get inspired by the feats of some of the world's greatest leaders and thinkers at the **Nobelmuseet**. (pictured, p45)

Dance away your blues to the sounds of one of Sweden's greatest cultural contributions to the world at **ABBA: The Museum**. (p85)

Right: Fotografiska (p90)

Fotografiska
THE MUSEUM OF PHOTOGRAPHY
IRVING PENN
LIKE A HORSE
AKSELI VALMUNEN
MAGNUS WENNMAN
OPEN SUN - WED 9AM - 11PM
THURS - SAT 9AM - 01AM

THE BEST

Outdoor Experiences

You're never too far away from the open air in Stockholm, and if you're looking for an active visit, this is a great place to do it.

Enter through the gates at **Blå Porten** and see why the large grounds of Djurgården were once a royal playground. (pictured, p76)

Rent a kayak and cruise down the river and past the smaller islands at **Långholmen**. (p95)

Stretch your legs as you enjoy the quirky buildings of **Hagaparken**. (p131)

Meander through the lungs of Stockholm in the greens of the **Ladugårdsgärdet** quarter. (p108)

Top up your tan at **Smedsuddsbadet** beach and cap off your visit with a quick ramble through the adjacent trail. (pictured, p122)

Rent a bike or lace up your running shoes and join countless fitness enthusiasts getting their miles in at **Tantolunden**. (p97)

Right: Kayaking, between Långholmen and Södermalm (p95)

THE BEST

Royal Experiences

Sweden's royals have a strong footprint throughout the capital and royal watchers will be rewarded pretty much anywhere they go.

Experience the grandeur and flamboyance of one of Europe's best known royal families at **Kungliga Slottet**. (p38)

Escape the city and wander through the palace and grounds of the royal country residence at **Drottningholm Slott**. (pictured, p21)

Wander around a stunning monument to regal whimsy and urban nature at the **Hagaparken**. (p130)

Learn some of the complex religious history of Sweden's royals at the breathtaking **Riddarholmskyrkan**. (p43)

Gasp at the gilded glamour of the Golden Room at the **Operan**. (pictured, p54)

Right: Riddarholmskyrkan (p43)

THE BEST

Gallery Experiences

Sometimes the best things come in small sizes, like Stockholm's galleries and museums.

Learn more about Sweden's most acclaimed children's author at her home, now turned into the **Astrid Lindgren's Hem** museum. (pictured, p136)

Revel in the celebration of art and love that is the **Millesgården**. (p111)

Marvel in the artistic inheritance gifted to the city by one of its most prolific royal collectors at the **Prins Eugens Waldemarsudde**. (pictured, p83)

Wander through the casts and prototypes in the studio of one of Sweden's best-known sculptors at the **Carl Eldhs Ateljémuseum**. (p136)

Right: Carl Eldhs Ateljémuseum (p136)

THE BEST

Viking Experiences

Scandinavia's largest city is also home to many attractions dedicated to the region's greatest explorers.

Learn the truth about one of the world's most mythical eras at installations dedicated to the Viking Age at the **Historiska Museet**. (p104)

Dance between myth and reality at the **Viking Museum**. (pictured, p78)

Ramble through the streets of Gamla Stan in search of **U 53** (p30), Stockholm's iconic rune stone.

Search the streets of the open-air **Skansen** museum to experience Viking-era exhibitions. (pictured, p85)

FROM LEFT: O.KEMPPAINEN/SHUTTERSTOCK ©, ANDREY SHCHERBUKHIN/SHUTTERSTOCK ©, XBRCHX/SHUTTERSTOCK ©

Kungliga Slottet (p38)

THE BEST

Architectural Experiences

The buildings of Stockholm are a dynamic monument to the various eras of history that have shaped the city, from tributes to royalty to celebrations of modern tastes.

Begin where Stockholm begins, at the seat of royal power in the majestic **Kungliga Slottet**. (p38)

Gasp at the striking details of Stockholm's seat of governance at the **Stadshuset** before relaxing in its small but delightful gardens. (p117)

Spend a day in the country enjoying the details and grandeur of **Drottningholm Slott**. (p21)

Embrace your inner Liberace with the gilded grandeur of the Golden Room at the **Operan**. (p54)

Go back in time with the classical buildings that surround the **Stortorget**. (p45)

THE BEST

Cycling Experiences

Stockholm's flat but generous sprawl lends itself to cycling (and running), as does the networks of cycle paths for all levels.

Rent a traditional Dutch bike at the **Royal Djurgården Visitor Center** and explore the many artistic gems that the island has to offer. (p150)

Make your way through the countryside out to the **Drottningholm Slott** alongside the water. (p132)

The path around Kungsholmen rewards walkers with stunning sunsets at **Fredhällsbadet** and **Smedsuddsbadet**. (p122)

From Östermalm, meander slowly towards the island of **Lidingö** to experience the chill of Stockholm's suburbs. (p111)

Connect the dots between Djurgården and Hagaparken through the **Royal National City Park**. (p130)

Cycling, Stockholm

ZKRAFT STOFF/SHUTTERSTOCK ©

Best for Kids

Inspire greatness in the youngest in your party by tracing the lives of Nobel Prize recipients at the **Nobelmuseet**. (p45)

Delight youngsters with a day at **Junibacken**. (p80)

Cool off in the waters off **Tantolunden** with a swim in the ocean on a hot summer day. (p97)

Enjoy the interactive animal demonstrations at the **Skansen Akvariet**. (p78)

Learn, discover and explore in the interactive installations at the **Tekniska Museet**. (p110)

Best for Free

Unravel the hidden and not-so-hidden secrets that make up the history of the city at the **Stadsmuseet**. (p94)

Enjoy the permanent installations at the **Nationalmuseum**. (p61)

Revel in the folly of royalty amongst the quirky buildings and delightful landscapes in the **Hagaparken**. (p130)

Wander through the trails and find all the sculptures in the lush **Djurgården**. (p150)

Enjoy the breathtaking sunset with a long stroll along the trail that links the **Stadshuset** (p117) to the **Rålambshovsparken**. (p122)

Take in the views of the old town from the highest point of Södermalm at **Monteliusvägen**. (p93)

Perfect Days

Get up early and head towards your nearest *bageri* (bakery) for a *fika* (coffee and pastry) before lacing up your walking shoes and enjoying the best of Stockholm.

Pastries in a Stockholm bakery

DAY ONE

Only Have One Day?

MORNING

Start at Gamla Stan tunnelbana (metro) station and follow the brown and yellow signs to the **Kungliga Slottet** (p38). Meander towards the **Stortorget** (p45) for the **Nobelmuseet** (p45) and lunch at the **Grillska Husets Konditori** (p48).

AFTERNOON

After witnessing the changing of the guard, wander towards Kungsholmen for the **Stadshuset** (p117). Spend some time down by the water for a view of the sunset.

EVENING

Head to Södermalm (pictured) beginning at **Monteliusvägen** (p93) for views over Gamla Stan, followed by dinner or joining the locals for a sip at a bar.

DAY TWO

A Weekend Trip

MORNING

Start at the **Nationalmuseum** (p61) for a quick lesson in the making of modern Sweden. Amble to **ABBA: The Museum** (pictured, p79) for a completely different history lesson on the origins of pop music.

AFTERNOON

Head to the **Royal Djurgården Visitor Center** (p150) and go on our cycling tour of the island to see how many of the impressive sculptures you can find. Pop by the **Moderna Museet** (p74) on Skeppsholmen to experience cutting-edge modern art.

EVENING

Head to the **Östermalms Saluhall** (p110) for a Swedish dinner in one of Stockholm's iconic spaces.

DAY THREE

A Short Break

MORNING

Take a tour of the **Tekniska Museet** (p110) and then visit the **Historiska Museet** (p114) for a history lesson.

AFTERNOON

Take a tour of the **Operan** (p54), including the majestic Golden Foyer, followed by a wander through the **Kungsträgården** (p54) before grabbing a quick lunch at the **Hötorgshallen** (p60).

EVENING

Make your way to Vasastan for a quick visit to the **Gustav Vasa Kyrka** (p139) or a wander through the **Sven-Harrys Konstmuseum** (p137). In the summer, take an early evening stroll through the **Hagaparken** (pictured, p130).

If You Have More Time

Head to **Långholmen** (p95) for a quick tour of Stockholm's past, including its quaint houses frozen in time. Take a dip in the lake at the **Långholmsbadet** (p95), if the weather permits, or drop in on the **Långholmen Prison Museum** (p95).

Learn more about the many indigenous and contemporary cultures that make up modern Scandinavia at the **Nordiska Museet (p78)** Add to your tour by visiting the **Etnografiska Museet (p110)** and the **Medelhavsmuseet** (p57) for exhibits that explore how Sweden sees itself. Visit the **Stadsmuseet (62)** for deeper insight into Stockholm itself.

Wander through **Skansen (p69)**, the open-air museum on Djurgården celebrating Sweden's past and crafts. Include a stop at the **Vasamuseet (p72)**, the most visited museum in Sweden, where you can really get up close to these intricately craved vessels.

Långholmen (p95)

BEN MEADOW/SHUTTERSTOCK ©

A City Day Trip

After your morning *fika*, take the bus out to **Drottningholm Slott** (pictured, p132) to enjoy the splendour of one of Stockholm's most magnificent castles. Don't skip the magnificent gardens or the Chinese Pavilion, and maybe catch a tour explaining how the site has transformed through the various generations of Swedish royals.

Grab a ferry from Slussen Ferry Terminal or Klara Mälarstrand and head one of the **outer islands** (p122) of the archipelago. Try to stay for dinner so you can enjoy the ferry back as a low-cost sunset cruise, including breathtaking sunset views over the water.

On a Rainy Day

Dance away your rainy day blues at **ABBA: The Museum** (p79). Catch a photography exhibition at **Fotografiska (p90),** followed by lunch or dinner at their award-winning restaurant.

Spend a morning at the **Kungliga Slottet** (p38) and the nearby **Livrustkammaren** (pictured, p39), before wandering to the **Nobelmuseet** (p45). Grab tea and a snack at the **Grillska Husets Konditori** (p48).

Get Prepared

BOOK AHEAD

Three months before
If you're visiting for an event such as the Stockholm Marathon or a concert at the Friend's Arena, book accommodation in advance.

One month before
Flight prices to and from Stockholm from other European capitals hit a sweet spot about a month before travel.

One week before
Reservations for dinner at any of Stockholm's award winning restaurants is best secured about a week in advance.

Manners Matter

Loud conversations on the train, tunnelbana (metro) or bus will generally be met with examining looks. Children are of course exempt and encouraged to be loud in their enjoyment of the city. Avoid walking on cycle paths as many people are commuting and not just cycling for fun.

There's a charge for shopping bags at most places – carry a tote bag with you if you're planning to buy things.

Money, Money, Money

Sweden is a card-first country, meaning that credit cards or digital payments are the preferred method of purchasing things across the city. In some places, it's not just a preference – cash won't be accepted and it's difficult to know when this may happen. So forget about changing money at the airport and instead plan around using a card. Most cards will also work on public transport.

Things to Know

Sweden does not use the euro! The krona is the official currency and it is very strong compared to most other currencies, so the prices of some everyday things might sting a little bit. Focus on the quality instead for your own peace of mind.

If you're not at a bar you can only buy alcohol at a Systembolaget (state-owned liquor store). There are quite a few distributed across town with identical logos so they should be easy to find, but remember, they close early in the afternoon on Saturday and reopen on Monday.

Many of the attractions in Stockholm have concessions for students, senior visitors and children. Look on the website before you go or ask at reception when you arrive. If you have a valid student card, you can also get a 50% discount on the weekly travel card.

TIPPING

Tipping isn't expected but is welcomed, although a service charge is often already included in the final bill.

- **10%+ — Restaurants & cocktail bars**: 10% for excellent service
- **0–10% — Other bars & cafes**
- **0–10% — Taxis**
- **0–10% — Hotel staff**

DAILY BUDGET

Budget: Less than 2000kr

- Bed in a budget hostel: **230kr**
- Ramen at a noodle bar: **210kr**
- Museum admission fee: **130–160kr but sometimes free**
- Public transport cap per day: **175kr**

Midrange: 2000–5000kr

- Double room with bathroom: **1640–2700kr**
- Two-course dinner with wine: **250–300kr**
- Guided tour of a museum: **150–250kr**
- Opera ticket: **260–670kr**

Top End: More than 5000kr

- Upmarket apartment or top-end hotel: **2700–4400kr**
- Dinner at a top restaurant: **540–1100kr**
- Premium opera ticket: from **850–1700kr**
- Island-hopping on a private boat: **10,000kr per week**

Currency
Krona (kr)

Language
Swedish

Time
Central European Time (GMT/UTC+1 in winter, GMT/UTC+2 during the daylight savings period)

TIP

If you're staying longer than five days, the weekly travel card is a great investment. It covers all means of transport including some of the archipelago.

When to Go

Stockholm sits on the water and has the variable weather to prove it – even in summer, temperatures can dip dramatically. Always pack a jumper.

There's no way to sugarcoat it: winters in Stockholm can be grim with grey weather. Snow quickly turns to sleet and put a damper on winter frolicking. Stockholmers generally soldier through these conditions in anticipation of the summer when every open space becomes a beach. Summer is the best time to visit. And while crowds can be a little daunting in places like Gamla Stan, the rest of the city remains pleasant and accessible at this time of year.

The Big Events

July: The largest pride festival in Europe is **Stockholm Pride** (p148), which is as much a celebration of LGBTIQ+ culture as it is of Sweden's impeccable pedigree in pop music.

August: Music, dance and other performances come together at the **Kulturfestivalen** (p62), a free festival that runs over several days in August across multiple venues.

August: If you're looking for a fast, flat course to chase a new personal best, the **Stockholm Marathon** is a great race for you. The half marathon is equally rewarding.

August/September: The **Stockholm Fringe Festival** (p94) is a multidisciplinary celebration of experimental art that happens across several stages over a week in the late summer. Much of it is in Swedish, but look out for the programme to see what might be available in English.

Stockholm Weather

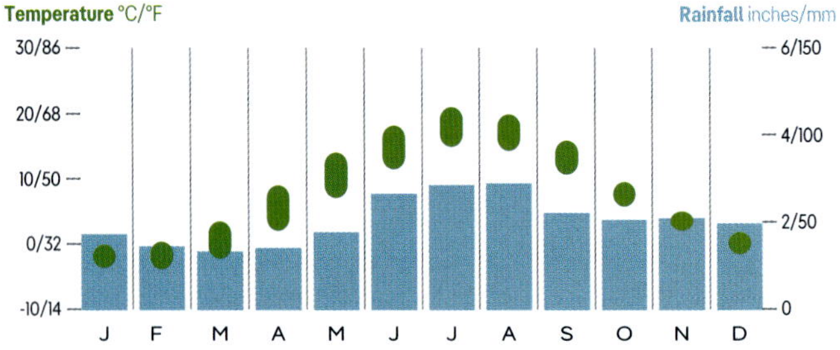

Stockholm Pride (p148)

Off the Beaten Path

April: For one night in April, nerds of the world convene at the **Kulturnatt Stockholm** (p96) where museums, libraries and other cultural sites stay open late and charge no admission fees. A delight for the mind and spirit.

October/November: **Restaurant week** (p62), or Dining Week as it is known in Stockholm, happens later in the year and features set menus at many of the city's great restaurants.

November: Over a million lights go up across Stockholm in November in preparation for Christmas at the **Stockholm Christmas Lights Festival**.

December: As if to lift away the gloom of the winter months, the **Nobelmuseet** (p45) invites light artists from around the world to put light displays on the facades of buildings and streets across the city.

ACCOMMODATION LOWDOWN

It's cheaper to stay in a hotel, especially in the low season, rather than in a private home rental. Look at outlying neighbourhoods as well because the city is so well served by public transport – you can stay in a five-star hotel in Solna or Ulriksdal for about half of what you'd pay for a private home in Södermalm.

Getting There

There are four airports that serve Stockholm, each with varying distances to the city centre. Check which airport you're flying into before committing to a ticket!

From the Airport to the City Centre

By Train

Arlanda Airport, Stockholm's main airport, is officially 28 to 35 minutes from the city centre, although this varies considerably depending on traffic. The Arlanda Express is a direct service that runs every 15 minutes (340kr one way). The commuter rail also runs into central Stockholm (186kr), but stops several times along the way.

Skavsta Airport is about 100km (two hours) from central Stockholm. Bus 515 takes you to the Nyköping rail station from where you can catch a direct train to Stockholm (100kr for a combined ticket).

Västerås Airport has no rail connections to central Stockholm, while Bromma Airport mostly serves regional flights to Malmö and Gothenburg.

By Bus

The Flygbussarna bus (149kr) runs every 10 to 15 minutes from Arlanda Airport. Flygbussarna also runs a service from Skavsta Airport (139kr), and from the other Stockholm airports. Tickets are available directly from the website (flygbussarna.se), and can also be bought on the bus with a debit or credit card (no cash).

By Taxi

Taxis into central Stockholm are an expensive proposition. Fares from Arlanda start at 695kr (30 minutes) while those from Skavsta start at 1500kr.

Other Points of Entry

If you're on an epic, trans-European adventure, you might consider taking the ferry from Helsinki in Finland to Stockholm (or in reverse). Tallink Silja Line (seven times per week) and Viking Line (pictured, six times per week) ferries both take approximately 18 hours between both towns, and cost around 1780kr.

EKATERINA POKROVSKY/SHUTTERSTOCK ©

Getting Around

Stockholm is small enough – and with dedicated cycle paths and pedestrian walkways – that walking or cycling are extremely reliable ways of getting around. But the city is also well served by multiple modes of transport. If you're staying for more than five days, buy the weekly pass.

Tunnelbana

Sweden's metro network, the *tunnelbana* (pictured), serves almost the entire city. Its three lines, covering seven routes, are known by their colours (green, red and blue). Check what the end station is on the route before you board because the same colour line can have different routes. All routes connect at the city's main train station, Centralstationen. A single ticket is valid for 75 minutes across the network (42kr). Trains run until 1am on weekdays and 3am on weekends. Pay attention to the details in the stations – Stockholm's *tunnelbana* network is known as the world's longest art gallery.

Commuter Rail

The Commuter rail network in Stockholm goes further into the suburbs and beyond than the tunnelbana and is a great option for travelling to outlying districts. Tickets are valid across both networks and interchange is easy.

All of the Commuter rail stations are also accessible by wheelchair and convenient for those who are travelling with luggage.

FROM LEFT: 9ROBOT/SHUTTERSTOCK ©, SCHAGER/SHUTTERSTOCK ©

ESSENTIAL APP

The SL app is your go-to app for transport within Stockholm.

Bus

There are hundreds of bus lines across Stockholm and buses run around every 10 minutes (often more frequently). Stockholm's main bus interchanges are at Slussen and the main bus station, Cityterminalen.

The buses are a great option for outlying towns like Vaxholm and Drottningholm. Bus 69 connects many of Stockholm's attractions but costs the same as a regular bus! You can also use the Stockholm Sightseeing bus with a 24-hour ticket.

Trams

There is only one tram line in Stockholm, the 7, that connects Norrmalm to Djurgården from the main train station, Centralstationen. The SL travel card is valid on the tram.

Ferries

The ferry is a great way to connect with the archipelago.

There are three ferry lines often known as Line 1, Line 2 and Line 3. SL cards are valid on these ferries and frequencies vary – check the boards for details.

There are also ferries that connect outlying islands for which separate tickets are required in the summer, and month-long SL cards are only valid in the winter.

The main ferry terminus in Gamla Stan is at Slussen.

Taxis

Taxis are a very expensive way to get around Stockholm, in part because of the traffic but also because taxi fares in Sweden are not regulated.

Getting around by taxi is almost always unnecessary unless you're travelling between 3am and 5am on weekdays.

Base fares start at 45kr, with a waiting fee of 500kr. Fares increase late at night and on weekends.

Public Transport Essentials

Digital Payments

Cash is not accepted on almost any form of public transport in Stockholm; your best bet is to purchase an SL card (20kr) that is reusable indefinitely. You can then load travel cards or money on the card as needed. Digital payments using contactless cards and phone apps are also widely accepted and encouraged.

Daily & Weekly Caps

A single ticket (42kr) is valid for 75 minutes for unlimited trips across all modes of public transport within that time. If you're going to be making multiple trips on public transport, the weekly travel card is a better investment than multiple single cards.

Discounts & Concessions

Discounts are available for students with a valid student card, minors under seven, seniors and people with disabilities. Most station information points are manned and you can ask for these concessions there.

TRAVEL COSTS

42kr
Single travel card (valid for 75 minutes)

155kr
24-hour pass

310kr
72-hour pass

405kr
7-day pass

TIP

Parents with a buggy (pram) ride free on all Stockholm buses.

TICKETS

- A single journey ticket is valid for 75 minutes across all modes of transport within the network. Tickets are available at all tunneblana and commuter rail stations, and at tunneblana machines at all the major commuter bus stops.
- Drivers and operators are not allowed to receive cash but you can tap and pay with a contactless debit or credit card.
- Ferries to the outer islands are not part of the SL network so you will have to purchase a ticket on the boat.

TICKET ZONES

There are no ticket zones within the city and its suburbs – trips are measured by duration rather than by zone. Make your last change before the ticket expires.

A Few Surprises

Stockholm has a quiet energy that makes it easy to overlook some great gems that are hidden in plain sight. Move slowly, look up and you might notice something new.

Underground Art

Notice the walls along the platforms or in the entry area of Stockholm's **tunnelbana** (p27, metro) stations. Since 1957 artists from all over the world have been invited to turn the tunnelbana into a canvas for all kinds of installations.

Medieval Mysteries

The area known as Stockholm has been settled since at least the Iron Age. Probably the oldest relic is **U 53** (p43), a piece of rune stone embedded in the facade of a shop wall on the corner of Prästgatan and Kåkbrinken streets. Learn more about rune stones in the region at the **Stockholm City Museum** (p45).

What Is Swedish Food Anyway?

Owing to the significant presence of immigrant communities in the city, the food here is diverse and eclectic. Try the **fusion restaurants** wherever you can.

Bang for Your Buck!

If you're a museum junkie you can save a lot of money by buying the **Stockholm Pass** (*stockholm.net/activities/stockholm-pass*). Valid for one to five days, this pass allows entry to over 60 attractions across the city, and also grants free travel on tourist buses and boats during the duration of validity.

Thrifty!

Second-hand shopping and reusing is very much embedded in the culture of Stockholm. The best shops are in **Södermalm** (p99), but **Vasastan** (p141) and **Kungsholmen** (p127) also offer delights.

Wander Free!

A law known as '*allemansrätten*' basically means that you can hike, cycle and picnic freely anywhere (including private property with some restrictions), and if you've hired a boat, you can sail anywhere as long as it doesn't interfere with the plant and animal life in the area.

ENNO HALLEK 'RAINBOW', STADION SUBWAY, STOCKHOLM, 1973. MISTER KNIGHT/SHUTTERSTOCK ©

Underground art, Stadion tunnelbana station

ZUZANA HABEKOVA/SHUTTERSTOCK ©

U 53 (p43)

Explore Stockholm

Stockholm Walking Tours

View of Stockholm from Mariaberget (p93)
MORGAN SODERSTROM/ISTOCK PHOTO ©

See p48
for eating, drinking and shopping listings

Explore
Gamla Stan

Gamla Stan is the centre of Stockholm's past and present. Dominated by the mammoth Kungliga Slottet (royal palace), Stockholm's historic birthplace also packs in Renaissance churches, fascinating museums and romantic squares. Gamla Stan includes two islets: Helgeandsholme, home to Sweden's parliament; and Riddarholmen, location of Riddarholmskyrkan, the royal necropolis; but everything is accessible via a short walk. Side streets offer up cute cafes for a quick *fika* (coffee and pastry) or large taverns where you can get your fix of traditional Swedish food. If you're trying to see Stockholm in a hurry, this is a great place to spend a whole day or at least a morning.

Getting Around

Bus

Most buses arrive at Slussen, and Gamla Stan is a short walk away. Line 53 from T-Centralen (3 minutes) will get you closest at Riddarhustorget.

Metro

Gamla Stan tunnelbana (metro) station is closest and there are clear signs to nearby attractions.

Walk

From Södermalm, walk towards Hornsgatan and Slussen. From Kungsholmen, the crossing is close to the Stadshuset.

★

THE BEST

ARCHITECTURAL WONDER
Kungliga Slottet (p38)

HISTORIC SQUARE
Stortorget (p45)

SWEDISH FOOD
Grillska Husets Konditori (p48)

HISTORICAL CHURCH
Riddarholmskyrkan (p43)

SHOPPING STREET
Köpmangatan (p47)

Gamla Stan
ROBERTO RIZZI/SHUTTERSTOCK ©

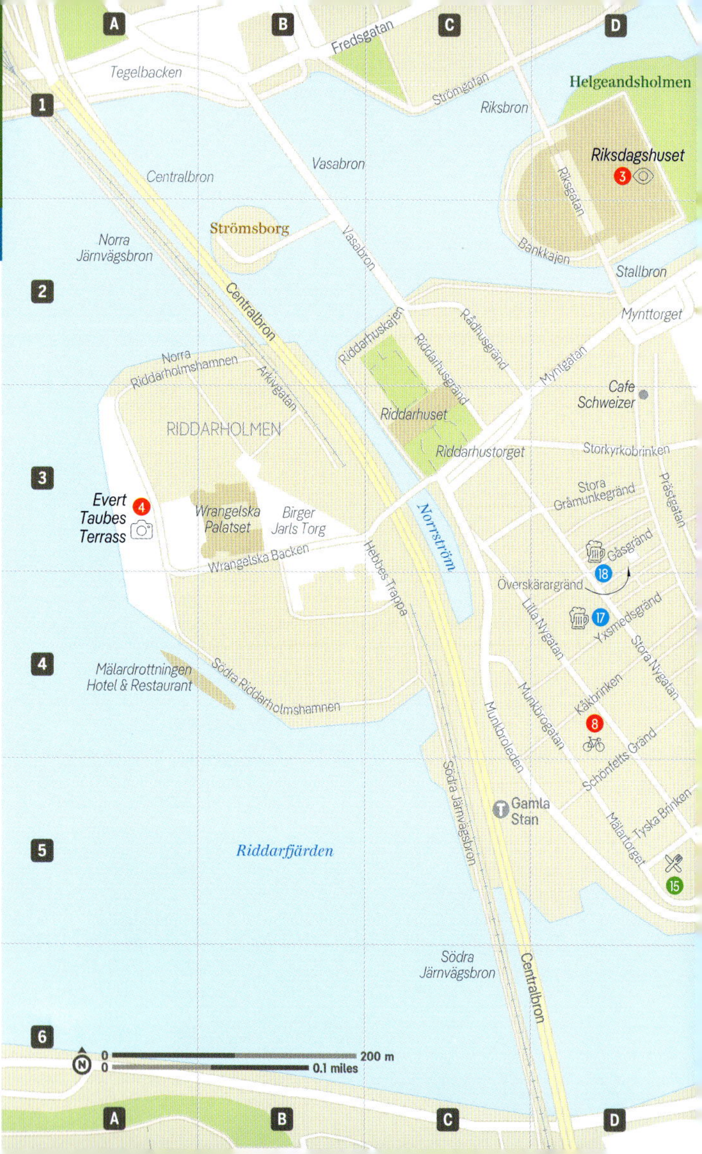
Tegelbacken
Fredsgatan
Strömgatan
Riksbron
Helgeandsholmen
Riksdagshuset
3
Riksgatan
Vasabron
Centralbron
Strömsborg
Norra Järnvägsbron
Bankkajen
Stallbron
Mynttorget
Rådhusgränd
Riddarhuskajen
Riddarhusgränd
Norra Riddarholmshamnen
Arkivgatan
Myntgatan
Cafe Schweizer
RIDDARHOLMEN
Riddarhuset
Riddarhustorget
Storkyrkobrinken
Prästgatan
Stora Gråmunkegränd
Evert Taubes Terrass
4
Wrangelska Palatset
Birger Jarls Torg
Norrström
Gåsgränd
18
Wrangelska Backen
Hebbes Trappa
Överskärargränd
17
Lilla Nygatan
Yxsmedsgränd
Stora Nygatan
Mälardrottningen Hotel & Restaurant
Södra Riddarholmshamnen
Munkbrogatan
Kåkbrinken
8
Munkbroleden
Schönfelts Gränd
Södra Järnvägsbron
Gamla Stan
Tyska Brinken
Mälartorget
Riddarfjärden
15
Södra Järnvägsbron
Centralbron
0
200 m
0
0.1 miles
A
B
C
D
1
2
3
4
5
6

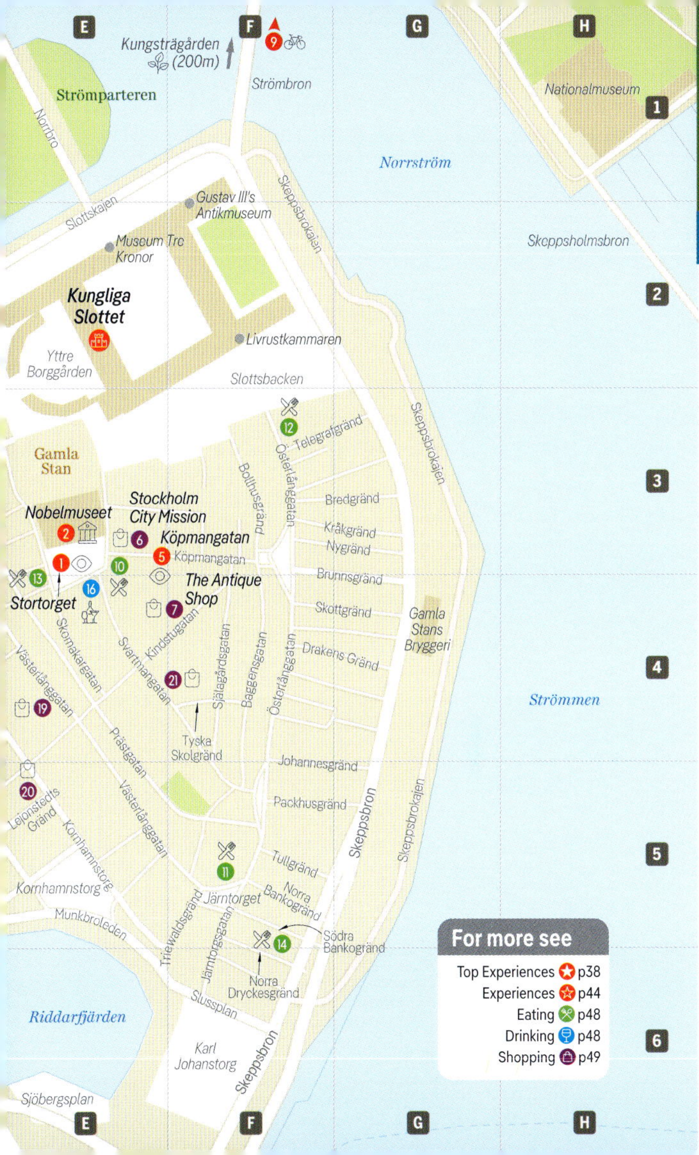
E
F
G
H
Kungsträgården (200m)
Strömbron
Strömparteren
Norrbro
Nationalmuseum
Norrström
Skeppsbrokajen
Gustav III's Antikmuseum
Slottskajen
Museum Tre Kronor
Skeppsholmsbron
Kungliga Slottet
Yttre Borggården
Livrustkammaren
Slottsbacken
Telegrafgränd
Gamla Stan
Bollhusgränd
Österlånggatan
Bredgränd
Stockholm City Mission
Nobelmuseet
Köpmangatan
Kråkgränd
Nygränd
Brunnsgränd
The Antique Shop
Stortorget
Skottgränd
Gamla Stans Bryggeri
Kindstugatan
Skomakargatan
Svartmangatan
Själagårdsgatan
Baggensgatan
Drakens Gränd
Västerlånggatan
Strömmen
Tyska Skolgränd
Prästgatan
Johannesgränd
Lejonstedts Gränd
Packhusgränd
Västerlånggatan
Kornhamnstorg
Skeppsbron
Skeppsbrokajen
Tullgränd
Järntorget
Norra Bankogränd
Munkbroleden
Triewaldsgränd
Järntorgsgatan
Södra Bankogränd
Norra Dryckesgränd
Slussplan
Riddarfjärden
Karl Johanstorg
Skeppsbron
Sjöbergsplan
For more see
Top Experiences p38
Experiences p44
Eating p48
Drinking p48
Shopping p49

★ TOP EXPERIENCE

Kungliga Slottet

Built on the ruins of the medieval Tre Kronor castle that burned down in 1697, the 608-room **Kungliga Slottet** palace is still used for its original purpose as the home of Sweden's royal family.

MAP P37 **E2**

PLANNING TIP
A combined ticket is available that also covers entry to Riddarholmskyrkan, but you can also buy a separate tickets. Concessions are available.

Royal Apartments

The Royal Apartments are the highlight of the tour of Kungliga Slotten, with their ornate, gilded interiors. Take a few moments in the glittering Karl XI Gallery, inspired by Versailles' Hall of Mirrors with its sparkling chandeliers, or at Queen Kristina's silver throne in the Hall of State. There's also an impressive collection of royal portraits from different eras that should satisfy any art lovers in your party. Note that the rooms in the Royal Apartments are still in somewhat regular use so they may be closed during certain events or periods – always check ahead.

Royal Treasury

Deep in the vaults of the palace is the Royal Treasury featuring the crown's most prized jewels and finery. Like royalty everywhere, the Swedish royals love a good hat and many of the crowns still in use for official occasions are on display here.

Gustav III's Antikmuseum

One of the oldest museums in the world, Gustav III's Antikmuseum (Museum of Antiquities) displays artefacts that are testament to the passions of King Gustav III, particularly from his travels to Italy. The collection features sculptures set in two stone galleries of stark tones that evoke being in a mausoleum, albeit with stunning views of the nearby courtyard. The museum's app contains more information about the individual sculptures. The museum is only open during the summer months (except for prebooked group tours).

Scan this code for information about tickets.

TRABANTOS/SHUTTERSTOCK ©

Royal Chapel

This chapel has allowed Swedish royals to pray without being surrounded by commoners since the 1700s, although there has been a chapel on the grounds since the 12th century. The gilded interiors and imposing sculptures showcase the talents of the architects and artists of various eras who were invited to showcase the might of the Swedish court, surrounded by hostile neighbours. Visit the chapel as part of the tour; also anyone can attend Sunday services here alongside palace staff.

Livrustkammaren

The Royal Armoury, also known as the Livrustkammaren, will be particularly compelling to royal watchers for its curious collection of memorabilia. Accessed off Slottsbacken, in the lofty vaults of the palace, the museum contains over 500 years

QUICK BREAK

Cafe Schweizer has been going for more than a hundred years. The freshly squeezed orange juice here is a great pick-me-up.

A ROYAL WALK
You can also book a walking tour around the exterior of the royal palace that emphasises its architectural and historical elements. Ask at the reception.

of royal history illustrated through unique items. Regal memorabilia on display includes Princess Sofia Magdalena's brocade wedding dress; Gustav II Adolf's stuffed battle steed, Streiff; the bloody linen cloth that was wrapped around the same monarch's heart by his grieving widow; and the tunic Gustav III was wearing on the night he was shot at the opera in 1792. The museum also features a collection of carriages used by royals through time. Read the descriptions and don't miss the gilded ceremonial coaches on the lower floor. With plenty of interactive elements and fun special exhibitions, the museum is particularly well set up to entertain kids.

Museum Tre Kronor

The Museum Tre Kronor (Three Crowns Museum) is a section of the palace's northern wing that is dedicated to the original Viking fort that sat on the same grounds as the palace today. It was unfortunately destroyed in a fire in the 17th century, but some recovered objects that survived are displayed here. The permanent installations include a selection of artefacts and replicas from various eras of the palace's history, as well as preserved sections of some of the earliest walls and paintings from the site.

Practicalities

Admission to the palace also includes the Museum Tre Kronor, the Royal Treasury and Gustav III's Antikmuseum (only open in the summer months). The guided tour is a great choice but you can also download an app that will give you abridged context about what you're looking at in the museum; particularly useful as some of the artefacts are not labelled.

Kungliga Slottet

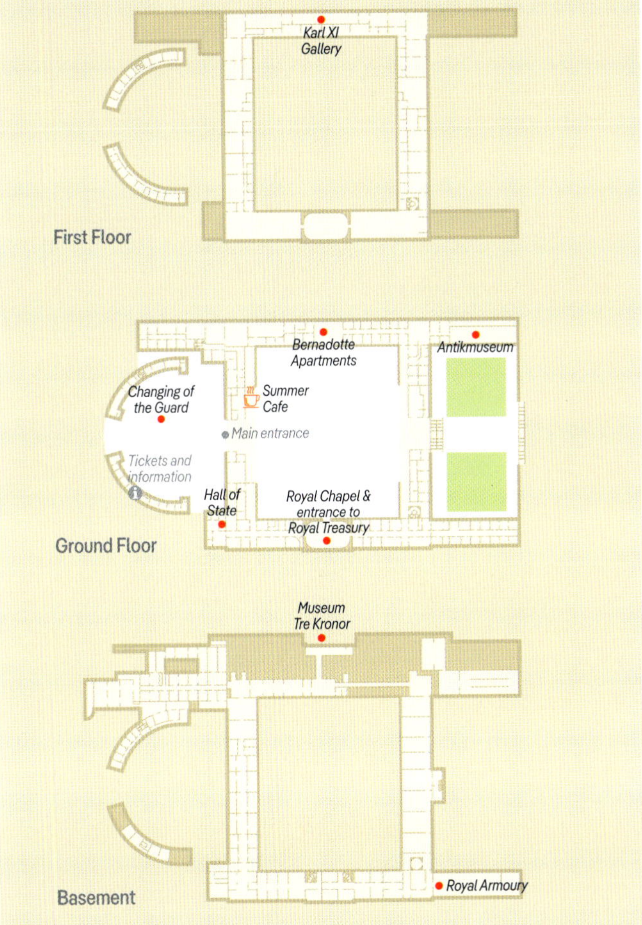

WALKING TOUR

Gamla Stan

In Gamla Stan's back alleys and quieter side streets, it can seem like Stockholm is almost unchanged since medieval times. If you don't go into any of the museums, you can get a flavour of the island in a few hours.

START	END	LENGTH
Riddarholmskyrkan	Sundsberg Konditiori	1km; two to three hours

1 Riddarholmskyrkan

From Gamla Stan station head to the small island of Riddarholms and the **Riddarholmskyrkan**, a church where all Swedish royals but one have been buried since the 17th century. The cavernous Gothic-style building is the only perfectly preserved church of its time, and a marker of Sweden's long history. The detailed paintings of the coat of arms along the walls are the coat of arms of the various knights of the Order of the Seraphim that serve the king, while gilded details sparkle over the tombstones of various kings and queens. A ticket to the Kungliga Slottet (p38) gets you entry to the church, but you can also buy a separate ticket.

2 Riddarhuset

Cross the bridge and head towards the **Riddarhuset**, or the House of Nobility (*riddarhuset.se*). This ornate 17th-century palace is where the Swedish nobility once gathered to govern the country. The statue in front is Axel Oxenstierna (1583–1654), an adviser to Queen Christina. The Riddarhuset was closed for renovation at the time of writing.

3 Storkyrkan

Take Storkyrkobriken towards **Storkyrkan** (the Great Church), a baroque building that is the main cathedral in the city and still used for royal weddings and coronations. Iy features a statue of St George and the Dragon. Head down Köpmangatan (Merchant's Street), browsing the shops, to reach the triangular 'square' at its end, where you'll find a replica of the St George and the Dragon statue on a plinth.

4 Stortorget

Swing by Gamla Stan's beautiful main square, **Stortorget** (p45), which was the location of the Stockholm Bloodbath of 1520. Surrounded by vividly coloured antique buildings, souvenir shops and cafes, it is tourist central. The cobbled square's grandest building is the former Stock Exchange, now home to the Nobelmuseet (p45). Swing by Kåkbinken for a quick glimpse of the U 53 rune stone, a 17th-century remnant of Stockholm's medieval past.

5 Mårten Trötzigs Gränd

Turn onto Västerlånggatan; on the right is **Mårten Trötzigs gränd**, a steep set of steps that connect to Prästgatan. At 35in across, this is one of the narrowest streets in Europe.

6 Sundsberg Konditiori

Right on Järntorget, a feature of Gamla Stan since the early 14th century is the bakery-cafe **Sundbergs Konditori** (p48); coffee has been served from the copper samovar here since 1785. Turn south on Triewaldsgra:nd and then east on Munkbroleden to head back to your starting point at Riddarholm.

EXPERIENCES

Kungsträgården CULTURAL VENUE

Kungsträgården (MAP: P36 E1) is the open area across the water from the Kungliga Slottet royal palace. There are regular events hosted here so it's worth walking past to see what's on. In the late summer, the park comes to life with the sights and sounds of Kulturfestivalen, the biggest cultural festival in Sweden, which is five days of food, music and fun. All of the festival's offerings are completely free as well so it's a great option for budget travellers. If you're visiting in the winter, Kungsträgården is where you'll find the city's open-air ice rink for some skating and mulled wine. It's also a great place to rest after a full day of walking and to get some great photos of the royal palace. Grab a sandwich and a drink, if the weather permits, and sit by the water for a few minutes.

Stockholm 1793 City Walk SELF-GUIDED TOUR

Sweden's long dark winters have fuelled an explosion of detective noir stories that are popular around the world. Stockholm native Niklas Natt och Dag is one of the top writers of the genre: his books have been translated into over 30 languages and are frequently number-one bestsellers in Stockholm and abroad. At the Stadsmuseum you can buy a map (40kr) that highlights key places featured in his books, providing an insight into 18th-century Stockholm. Visiting these places on a self-guided tour not only brings the cobblestone alleys of Gamla Stan to life but also allows you to learn more about some of the older buildings around the city whose significance might not be immediately apparent.

Stockholm Ghost Walk SPOOKY WALKING TOUR

It's hard not to conjure up thoughts of ghouls and spirits when walking through the narrow alleys of Gamla Stan, particularly in the winter when the days are dark and the mist rises from in between the cobblestones. The founders of **Stockholm Ghost Walk** (*stockholmghostwalk.com/en; adult/child 280/180kr*) picked up on this vibe and at 7pm on scheduled days, they guide visitors through the streets of Gamla Stan in search of spectres and spooks. For a city that welcomes most of its visitors in the summer, this could be a particularly interesting activity for anyone who's here in winter, especially over Halloween. The tour takes about 90 minutes and is mostly talking so they discourage children younger than seven who might be better entertained by more obvious delights.

Holiday Hunts at the Royal Palace CHILDREN'S ACTIVITIES

It can be hard to think up ways of entertaining children who are old enough to be curious but too young to spend three hours in a museum. Don't worry, the Kungliga Slottet (p38) has you covered. During the school holidays in Sweden, the royal palace hosts themed 'holiday hunts' that encourage children to interact with the artefacts and installations in various parts of the buildings. The hunts involve picking up a themed map at the entrance and exploring the Royal Apartments in search of specific paintings or images. Visitors can take the challenge at any time during their visit to the palace. Tickets include a small prize for all participants – check the calendar on the website (*kungligaslotten.se*) for details on when the next holiday hunt will be held.

Nobel Experiences TALKS/SPEECHES

MAP: 2 P36 **E3**

On Friday nights, the **Nobelmuseet** (*nobelprizemuseum.se/en; admission fee varies*) stays open until 9pm to allow visitors a chance to learn more about Nobel Prize winners, their work and their impact on the world. These events begin with a happy-hour style champagne reception at the museum bistro featuring a special menu that changes according to the seasons. After indulging in champagne and nibbles, attendees can then choose to attend a talk, a guided tour or even (occasionally) a music performance built around either that year's prize or a

THE OLDEST SQUARE IN THE CITY

It's easy to underestimate **Stortorget** because, if you don't know what you're looking at, you probably just see an open square. But this space has been the centre of Stockholm since the Middle Ages and is home to some of the most eclectic vintage architecture in the city. Look up to get a sense of how many people have gathered here over the centuries and built homes and businesses here. The history of Stortorget is not all champagne and roses – this is also the location of the Stockholm Bloodbath, a grisly event reminiscent of the Red Wedding in *Game of Thrones* when a member of the Danish royal family gathered other members of the nobility for a party that ended a little differently than they'd probably hoped or imagined. The aftermath of that dark chapter was Gustav Vasa mobilising his countrymen to overthrow the King, leading to the permanent independence of Sweden from Denmark. Learn more about the Stockholm Bloodbath at the **Stockholm City Museum** (*stadsmuseet.stockholm/en; free*). (MAP: 1 P36 **E3**)

theme that connects various prize winners. It's a great way to slow down and experience the museum. Events are held in both English and Swedish but run on specific schedules, so check the museum website before making firm plans. Special tickets are necessary and concessions are available for museum members.

Where the Rules Are Made

GUIDED TOUR

MAP: 3 P36 D1

Half of the island Helgeandsholmen is the **Riksdagshuset** (*riksdagen.se/en*; free), the Swedish Parliament. It is an impressive neo-baroque building with grand windows and lofty arches that seems to spill right into the water. The other half is Strömparterren, a public park and the gardens of the parliament – it's lush, green and particularly inviting in the summer. If you're interested in how laws are passed in Sweden, you may want to book into one of the guided tours that showcase the grand interiors of the Riksdagshuset and explain the complex dance between the monarchy, the legislature and the different regions that make up the territory. In the winter you can also attend tours that are specifically curated to showcase the significant art collection contained in the building. Tours are free but they do fill up quickly as only 28 slots are available each day and if you don't arrive on time they will give your slot to the next person in line.

A Walk to Remember

WALKING/CYCLING

Don't bother with car hire if you're only planning to stay in Stockholm! The city is well served by public transport and so small that everything is accessible if you have comfortable shoes and are not in a hurry. After you're done touring

BUILDING BRIDGES ACROSS THE WATER

The City of Stockholm is made up of 14 major islands and a number of small islets that have been knotted together over time to make up the modern city that we know today. What we think of as Gamla Stan is actually four islands – Stadsholmen is the main one with the majority of attractions; Riddarsholmen is where the Riddarholmskyrkan and other significant buildings lie; Helgeandsholmen is home to the parliament; and Strömsborg is a tiny islet only big enough for one moderately sized palace that today serves as the headquarters of an international organisation. It's hard to tell because the islands are so close together but just remember that the waters that flow between the buildings of Gamla Stan are not rivers or canals – it's the sea!

the major sites, make time to walk the perimeter of the islands, beginning in Stadsholmen. The western side of the island offers excellent views of Djugården and the open water beyond, while the northern side is the best place for photographs of the Riksdagshuset. From the Riksdagshuset, you get excellent views of almost the entire edifice of the Kungliga Slottet. And at sunset, wander down to the waterside on Riddarsholmen to the **Evert Taubes Terrass** (MAP: 4 P36 **A3**) for some of the most Instagrammable photos of the city. Sunsets in Stockholm are a drawn-out affair, particularly in summer, and this is also a great place to sit and contemplate amongst the sculptures and the views. Gamla Stan itself is best photographed from Södermalm.

Something Old, Something New

SHOPPING

Köpmangatan (MAP: 5 P36 **E3**) is the oldest named street in Stockholm and one of the best places to shop for knick-knacks, antiques and souvenirs. From high-end craft stores selling niche products made of fabric and fibres, to the **Stockholm City Mission** (MAP: 6 P36 **E3**) that sells second-hand and upcycled clothing and furniture to support the homeless throughout the city, this is a great place to buy something that has a little more meaning than the mass-produced objects you might find in other parts of the city. **The Antique Shop** (MAP: 7 P36 **F4**) is great for vintage homewares and tchotchkes.

BEST ALTERNATIVES TO WALKING

Gamla Stans Cykel

MAP: 8 P36 **D4**

(gamlastanscykel.se) Rent a three-speed bicycle for a speedier tour of the city from Gamla Stan's oldest bicycle shop. They don't do e-bikes.

Go Stockholm

MAP: 9 P36 **F1**

(gostockholm.se; 360kr) See Stockholm from the back of a low-emissions golf cart, with audio guides and supported by a tour guide. Wheelchair-friendly.

Voi

(voi.com/city/stockholm; starts at 3kr per min) Zip between stops with e-scooter rentals for adults in Stockholm. Remember that you're not allowed to leave your scooter on the pavement in Sweden!

LISTINGS

Best Places for...

See p36 for map of locations

€ Budget €€ Midrange €€€ Top End

Eating

Historical Dining

Grillska Husets Konditori €€
10 E3
Delicious tea, coffee, sandwiches and pastries with a fantastic view of the main square. The delicatessen is closed on weekends. *grillskahuset.se; 10am-7pm Mon, Fri & Sat, to 8pm Tue-Thu, 11am-7pm Sun*

Sundbergs Konditori €€
11 F5
Indulge in *fika* in one of the oldest coffee houses in Gamla Stan (pictured). Beware of the tourist crowds – this is a popular spot that requires some patience, but the cake is good. *9am-8pm Mon-Fri, from 10am Sat & Sun*

Tradition €€
12 F3
A great place to sample a traditional menu of Swedish classics like meatballs and reindeer blood pudding. Reservations recommended. *restaurangtradition.se; 5-11pm Thu-Sat, to 10pm Sun & Mon*

Kaffekopen €
13 E4
Another of Gamla Stan's 17th-century coffee houses offers hot and cold drinks with sandwiches and pastries in a building somewhat untouched by the passage of time, overlooking Stortoget. *cafekaffekoppen.se; 10am-10pm Sep-May, from 9am Jun-Aug*

Zum Franziskaner €€
14 F5
Traditional Swedish fair in a tavern that has been on the site since the beginning of the 20th century. A great stop for beer and ale lovers. *zumen.se; 4-11pm Mon, to midnight Tue-Thu, 3pm-midnight Fri & Sat, 3-11pm Sun*

Gamla Stans Fisk €€
15 D5
It would be absurd to travel all the way to Stockholm, surrounded by water, and leave without trying some fish. This is one of the most celebrated places in town to get your fix. *gamlastansfisk.se; 11am-4pm Tue-Fri*

Drinking

Stylish Sipping

Pharmarium
16 E4
Enjoy eclectic cocktails and nibbles at this Stockholm institution housed in the building where Stockholm's first pharmacy opened in 1575. Book ahead to be sure, but they do hold some tables for walk-ins. *pharmarium.se; 5-11pm Sun-Tue, 4pm-midnight Wed & Thu, 3pm-1am Fri & Sat*

Tritonia
17 D4
Travel around the world in 80 beers – well, 70 – at one of Gamla Stan's iconic brewhouses and tap rooms, including a

rotating selection of local microbrews. *tritonia.se; 4-11pm Tue-Thu, to midnight Fri, 3pm-midnight Sat*

Wirströms

18 D4

An Irish pub in Stockholm that still manages to serve plentiful Swedish food and drink. Live music on Tuesdays as well. *wirstromspub.se; 3pm-1am Mon-Fri, from noon Sat, noon-9pm Sun*

Shopping

Niche Delights

Science Fiction Bookshop

19 E4

A globally renowned destination for sci-fi lovers, this bookshop uses the genre label broadly. It's also a great place to stock up on games and related items. *sfbok.se; 10am-7pm*

Gamla Stans Polkagriskokeri

20 E5

Pick up your traditional Swedish sweets here, including peppermint candy and fudge made on site using traditional techniques. *gamlastanspolkagriskokeri.se; 10am-8pm*

Chaikhana

21 F4

Buck against the dominance of coffee and stock up on globally acclaimed tea varieties and unique local blends at this Stockholm institution that also has a great tea room attached. *chaikhana.se; 10am-7pm Wed-Fri, noon-6pm Sat & Sun*

See p65
for eating,
drinking and
shopping
listings

Explore Norrmalm

Norrmalm is the city's thoroughly modern commercial hub; both the main train and bus stations (Centralstationen and Cityterminalen, respectively) are located here. Indiscriminately bulldozed in the 1960s, the district claims some of the capital's most controversial architecture, most notably the five Hötorget buildings, lined up like 72m-tall dominoes. This is a great place to top up on hiking or camping gear, and if you're looking to pick up some fashion items or budget design pieces, there are many small shops that will delight. It's also home to cultural heavyweights like the Operan and the Nationalmuseum. The easiest way to navigate the area is to take public transport to the Centralstationen then just let the city unfold around you block by block.

Getting Around

Bus & Train

Both the main bus station (Cityterminalen) and the main train station (Centralstationen) are in Norrmalm, so any transport heading here will put you right at the heart of things.

Metro

Hötorget tunnelbana (metro) station puts you within walking distance of many of the central attractions of the neighbourhood, as does Centralstationen.

Walk

Norrmalm is easily walkable from Gamla Stan if you head north from the Kungliga Slottet, but you will have to cross one or two major roads. Obey the traffic signals.

THE BEST

ARCHITECTURAL WONDER
Operan (p54)

HISTORIC SQUARE
Hötorget (p58)

MUSEUM
Nationalmuseum (p61)

SMALL MUSEUM
Hallwylska Museet (p60)

SHOPPING STREET
Drottninggatan (p60)

Norrmalm

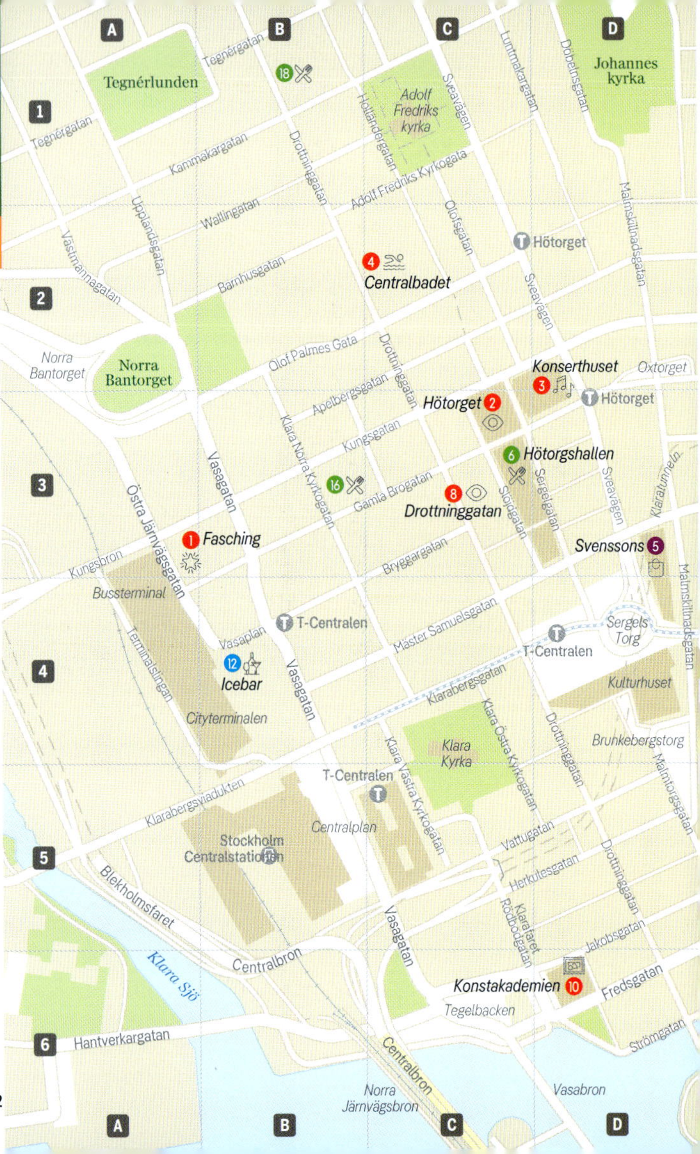
A
B
C
D
1
2
3
4
5
6
Tegnérlunden
Tegnérgatan
Adolf Fredriks kyrka
Johannes kyrka
Kammakargatan
Drottninggatan
Holländergatan
Sveavägen
Luntmakargatan
Döbelnsgatan
Adolf Fredriks Kyrkogata
Upplandsgatan
Wallingatan
Västmannagatan
Olofsgatan
Hötorget
Malmskillnadsgatan
4 Centralbadet
Barnhusgatan
Norra Bantorget
Olof Palmes Gata
Konserthuset 3
Oxtorget
Apelbergsgatan
Hötorget 2
Kungsgatan
6 Hötorgshallen
Klara Norra Kyrkogatan
16
Gamla Brogatan
8 Drottninggatan
Sergelgatan
Sibiggatan
Klaratunneln
Vasagatan
Östra Järnvägsgatan
1 Fasching
Svenssons 5
Kungsbron
Bryggargatan
Bussterminal
T-Centralen
Mäster Samuelsgatan
Sergels Torg
Vasaplan
Terminalslingan
12 Icebar
Klarabergsgatan
Kulturhuset
Cityterminalen
Klara Östra Kyrkogatan
Klara Kyrka
Brunkebergstorg
Malmtorgsgatan
Klara Västra Kyrkogatan
Klarabergsviadukten
Centralplan
Stockholm Centralstation
Vattugatan
Herkulesgatan
Blekholmsfaret
Rödbodgatan
Klarafaret
Jakobsgatan
Klara Sjö
Centralbron
Konstakademien 10
Fredsgatan
Tegelbacken
Hantverkargatan
Strömgatan
Norra Järnvägsbron
Vasabron
18

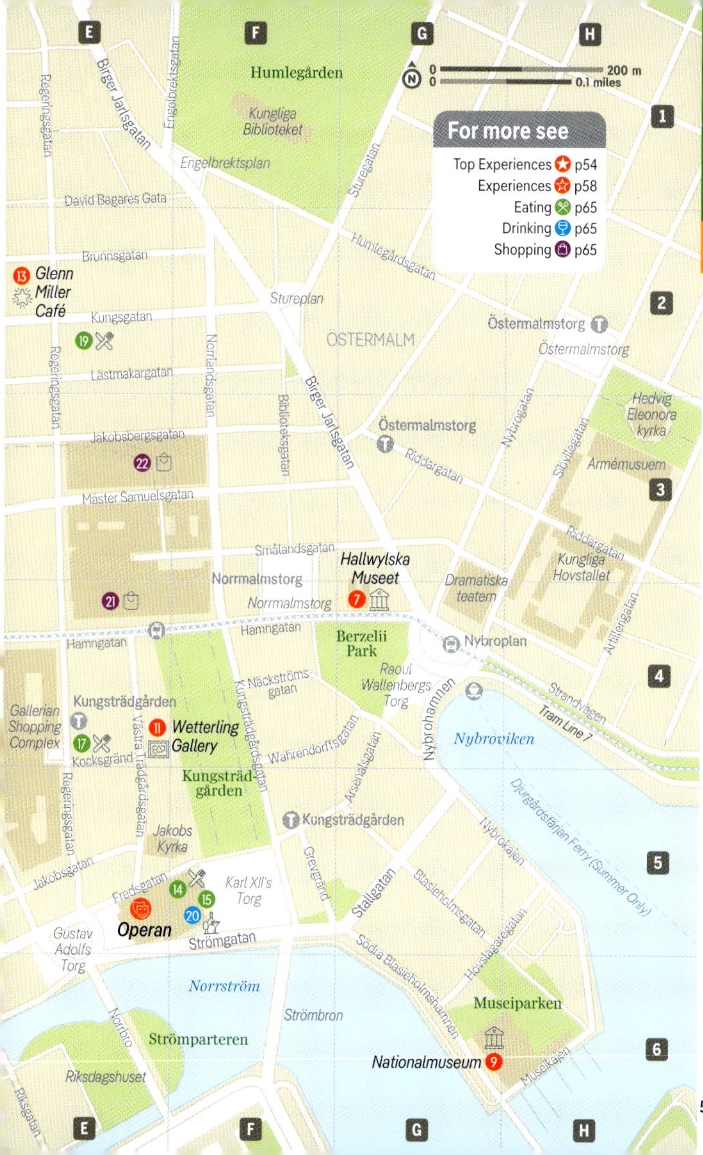

For more see
Top Experiences p54
Experiences p58
Eating p65
Drinking p65
Shopping p65

★ TOP EXPERIENCE

Operan

If opera is the music of kings then there can be no better place to bask in its glories than at the Kungliga Operan (or Royal Opera House) often simply known as **Operan**.

MAP P53 **E5**

PLANNING TIP
Guided tours of the opera house in English (120kr) are only available on Saturdays at 12.30pm and must be booked in advance on the website.

Scan this QR code to buy tickets for a guided tour.

Grand Entries

The Operan that you see today is the late-19th-century reconstruction as the original 1782 building was abandoned and finally demolished after the king was shot and later died while attending a masked ball there in 1792. Sightseeing tours will give you a short description of the exterior but don't rush through it if you can linger a while. Give the facade a few minutes, taking in the neoclassical elements including the elaborate entryway and the two-toned brick-and-mortar work. Once you enter, the architecture shifts tone into neo-baroque with elaborate paintwork and sparkling interiors. Notice the marble in the entry hall – it was specifically imported from neighbouring Norway as a gesture of unity.

Auditorium

The plush velvet and shiny marble of the grand entrance whisks you up towards the auditorium, the heart of the Operan. A good way to experience this impressive space is to start at eye level, taking in the stage as an audience member would before focusing on the ceiling details. And when you finally look up, spend some time on the details of the imagery, including the little angel carrying a painting of the architectural map of the Operan. The massive crystal-and-gilt chandelier that hovers imposingly over the room weighs an impressive 2 tonnes: a testament to the sturdiness of this building. At capacity, 1100 people can watch their favourite operas here but even when

KERT/SHUTTERSTOCK ©

empty, this is a space designed to take your breath away – give it time to do so.

Golden Foyer

The highlight of the opera tour is the Golden Foyer, or the Golden Stairwell. Neglected for years as the building fell into disrepair, this entryway was restored in 1989 to lift the nearly 100 years of dust and grime that had accumulated. The result? Breathtaking. Walking through the foyer feels like you're walking inside a crystal, surrounded by glistening and sparkling surfaces. But this is not just a walkway, it is also a performance venue, and smaller chamber music or solo performances are hosted here, usually free for ticket holders attending the opera that night. Check the opera's calendar to make sure you don't miss a bonus performance in this magnificent space.

QUICK BREAK
Operan guests are required to preorder their refreshments online or via the app in order to avoid the frustration of waiting in long queues during the performance intervals.

WALKING TOUR

Normalm

Normalm is one of the less pleasantly walkable areas, not because it doesn't have pavements and cycle paths, but because it is more brick and concrete than other parts of the city and involves crossing more major roads. This walking tour should give you a sense of the neighbourhood and its key landmarks.

START	END	LENGTH
Medelhavsmuseet	St Klara Kyrka	2km; two hours

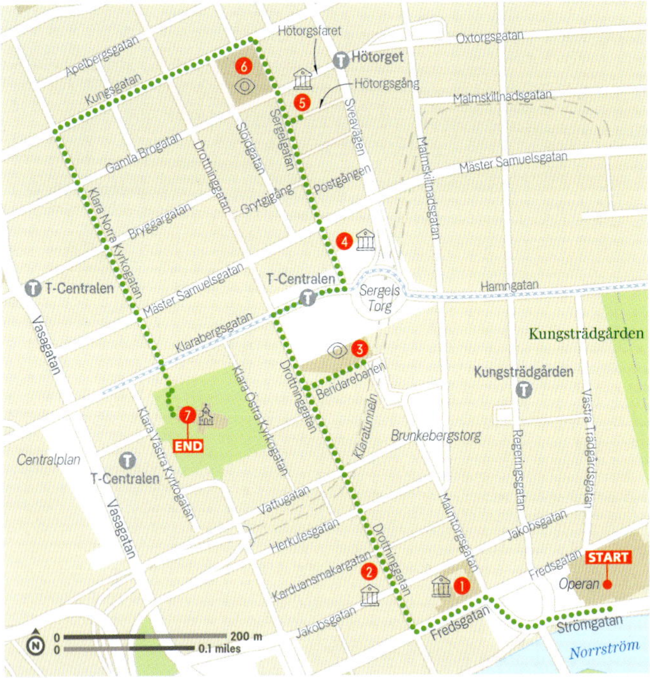

1 Medelhavsmuseet

Medelhavsmuseet (Museum of Mediterranean and Near Eastern Antiquities), a five-minute walk from Operan, is a great place to spend an entire morning learning from an institution that is trying to reckon with the role that museums play in taking important cultural objects from other parts of the world.

2 Dansmuseet

Head towards Drottninggatan for the **Dansmuseet** (Museum of Dance), a museum and performance space dedicated to the art of movement. There are permanent installations devoted to specific cultures and rotating special exhibitions around specific themes.

3 Kulturhuset

Stockholm's **Kulturhuset** boasts everything culture-related including performance spaces, cinema screens, a library and co-working spaces as well as a bookstore. Most of the offerings are in Swedish but it's an interesting architectural stop and a great place to people-watch Stockholmers in their element. If you're planning to stay in town a little longer, they also host a language cafe that allows you to practice your Swedish.

4 Avicii Experience

Commemorate the life of one of Sweden's most popular musicians whose life was cut short far too soon. Tim Bergling, also known as Avicii, was one of the brightest lights in dance and electronic music until he lost his battle with depression in 2018 at the age of 28. This **museum** is a tribute to his career and impact on the scene, and while the experience itself is small, it's a great stop for music lovers.

5 Paradox Museum

The **Paradox Museum** is a great stop to entertain the young and the young at heart for a few hours. Filled with optical illusions that challenge your sense of depth and perception, it will give you something to laugh about for the rest of your trip. Use the entrance at Sergelagatan as you make your way towards Hötorget, or access the entrance from Hötorget tunnelbana.

6 Hötorget

Walk down Sergelgatan towards **Hötorget** (p58), a town square that hosts a Sunday flea market as well as flower and food vendors. On other days it's mostly fruit and vegetables, but the surrounding restaurants are great place to take a short break or grab a meal.

7 St Klara Kyrka

This **church** is a great place to finish a tour because it regularly hosts free classical music performances in its cavernous nave, and it's right next to Centralstationen and great for transport connections.

EXPERIENCES

Dance it Out

LIVE MUSIC

MAP: 1 P52 **A3**

Fasching (*fasching.se; admission fee varies*) is an institution in Stockholm for a reason. Part nightclub, part restaurant, part performance space and all the way through an experience, this space is a great way to engage with contemporary Stockholm. There's also a restaurant that serves high-end bar food here. One of the oldest jazz venues in Sweden, Fasching regularly hosts performances by up-and-coming musicians – and jazz is huge in Stockholm so you're bound to be listening to someone interesting. The venue is also well-known for its themed club nights on Fridays and Saturdays throughout the year as well as special performances by touring musicians. Many of these events are 'pay to enter' and the price varies according to the performance, but if you're lucky you might catch one of the free sets that are occasionally played in the foyer. There's only one way to find out – go and see what's on. Adults only.

Life in the Square

MARKETS

MAP: 2 P52 **C3**

Hötorget is one of the main squares in Stockholm and home to its renowned flea market. Every Sunday vendors from across the city display their knick-knacks making it a great place to collect vintage items at decent price points. Hötorget is particularly well-known for the accessible art that is sold here by working painters: in fact, Hötorget art is a phrase used to refer to the kind of art that shows technique and talent but doesn't necessarily rise to the level of collectible. It's a good place to find something pretty to add to your home. On other days the market is mostly food and flower vendors until about 6pm when it empties out completely.

Noble Entertainments

ARCHITECTURE

MAP: 3 P52 **D2**

The most iconic part of Hötorget is the powder-blue building with the imposing pillars that overlooks the square. This is the **Konserthuset** (*konserthuset.se; adults/under-26s 100/55kr*), home to the Stockholm Philharmonic Orchestra. Every year on 10 December the concert hall is even more elevated in glitz and glamour as flowers are imported and textiles are added to commemorate the awarding of the Nobel Prizes, and classical music by the Philharmonic is also performed. If you didn't get your invitation to the prize ceremony this year, don't worry. You can still book a guided tour of the concert hall – with the main tour offered in Swedish, and English available through an audio guide – and watch the stream of the event online later on.

Too Hot to Trot

SAUNAS/SWIMMING POOLS

MAP: 4 P52 **C2**

You can't come to Sweden and not try a sauna. That may not be a law yet but it definitely feels like an unwritten rule. What better place to experience this most Swedish of experiences than the **Centralbadet** (central baths), where many Stockholmers come to indulge as well? This spa has been on the site since the beginning of the 20th century, offering a range of treatments and holistic interventions, and featuring five saunas and a swimming pool. The spa oozes luxury and even has its own range of products so you can take a little of the magic home with you. You do have to book and pay in advance on their website and a prebooked slot gets you three hours of access to all facilities except massages and fitness classes. There are off-peak prices for Monday to Thursday, and peak prices on the weekend.

Design Delights

SHOPPING

MAP: 5 P52 **D3**

IKEA is a great entry point, but the Swedes have been making great furniture for a lot longer than most of us have heard of the homewares giant. Norrmalm is home to some of Sweden's best-known furniture design shops and you can swing by either to test your baggage limits or to admire the handiworks of some of these great craftspeople. **Svenssons** (*svenssons.se*) on Sveavägen is one of the oldest furniture shops in the country, spread out over two floors and unfolding like a museum of modern interiors. The collections are curated from different designers and companies so there's a mix of various styles, each united by their quality and flair. Pick up some inspiration for your next home update here. You might not walk out with a sofa, but maybe you'll get a throw or a vase that will remind you of your time in Stockholm.

PUB: PAUL URBANUS BERGSTRÖM

The building with the word PUB in large letters across its main entrance is not a pub. Today it is a large hotel but in its heyday, this was one of the biggest department stores in Sweden founded by one Paul Urbanus Bergström. Opened in 1888 and conveniently located by Hötorget square where people were shopping anyway, the department store quickly became one of Stockholm's most frequented addresses. Film star Greta Garbo worked here before she left to attend film school and it was a popular place for high-level people from the Communist bloc to shop during the Cold War because Sweden was a neutral country where they could indulge in a little discreet capitalism.

Pick Your Pleasure

FOOD/DRINK

MAP: 6 P52 C3

Just off the Hötorget is the **Hötorgshallen**, a food hall offering a taste of contemporary Swedish and international cuisine. Spread across two floors, the food hall is made up of 40 independent vendors, many of whom have been on the site for decades, although some are international chains trying to benefit from the foot traffic. The food hall is particularly popular with office workers and the lack of dinner service reflects this – vendors shut at 6pm on the lower ground floor on weekends, and 7pm upstairs. But if you're swinging by for lunch you will be richly rewarded. **Hellbergs** (p65) on the lower ground floor has a menu that includes reindeer-blood pudding that is so much more delicious than it sounds, while **Kasja's Fish** has been serving fish and seafood at this location for over 30 years to great success. Vegans will also be satisfied with the offerings at **Ankara's Kebab**.

A Little Museum

MUSEUM

MAP: 7 P52 G4

The Hallwyl family left a huge cultural imprint on Stockholm – their grandson was the founder of the Dansmuseet – and the small **Hallwylska Museet** (*hallwylska museet.se; adult/child 120kr/free*) is a monument to the family's passion for collecting, especially Wilhelmina's. During her lifetime this noblewoman assembled an eclectic collection of objects and paintings that she rightly guessed would fascinate audiences long after she was gone: there's everything from paintings to things you might find in a toilet. The house itself is a marvel to walk through – wander the richly decorated rooms where the painstakingly catalogued items are beautifully displayed for a flavour of how the wealthy of their day would have lived. Tickets only cover two of the five floors and, unfortunately, there's no lift, making this one of Stockholm's least accessible museums.

Shop Until You Drop

SHOPPING

MAP: 8 P52 C3

Stretching almost the entire length of Norrmalm is the shopping street of **Drottninggatan**, which is one of the main shopping districts in Stockholm. Here you'll find every single modern shop that you can imagine and it's a great place to shop for affordable contemporary design in either fashion or homewares. Some of the names will be familiar – all the chains are represented – but you can also find some smaller niche stores. For glassware try **Måleras Glassworks**, while **Lager 157** is well-known in Scandiavia for offering high quality denim and winter wear at very affordable prices.

History Lives Here

MUSEUM

MAP: 9 P52 G6

The **Nationalmuseum** (*nationalmuseum.se; adult/under-20s 160kr/free*) is the largest collection of art and design objects in Sweden. The stunning building overlooks the water and is a natural stopping point if you're done with a tour of Gamla Stan or Djurgården. You could just come here and hang out in the coffee shop or the sculpture courtyard, which has a number of gems showcased there as well. But why deny yourself the amazing works throughout the rest of the building? This is one of those places where it's worth it to splurge on the audio guide. The collection is displayed chronologically but also narratively to highlight specific connections between various pieces. The sculpture garden, for example, tells the story of the shift from idealism to realism as sculptors began to put tremendous effort into breathing a sense of life and movement into marble. The focus is on European art and design so you may feel a keen silence about the rest of the world, but once you enter with that in mind, you will be rightly rewarded. Lovers of Swedish design will be particularly fascinated by the Design Depot, a section of the museum that showcases a selection of gorgeous objects that tell a story about how Swedish design has evolved over time.

High Art

GALLERY

MAP: 10 P52 D6

The Royal Academy of Fine Arts, **Konstakademien** (*konstakademien.se; admission free*), is the oldest academy in Sweden that hands out prizes and awards for various artistic academies in the country. It is housed in a beautiful neoclassical building on Fredsgatan, just by the large interchange, with a gallery space that celebrates the best in contemporary art. This is mostly modern and experimental art that is

NORRMALM OR DJURGÅRDEN?

The boundaries between Stockholm's various districts are a little arbitrary in part because it's such a compact town with only a few natural elements to act as boundaries. Södermalm, Långholmen and Kungsholmen are wholly ensconced on single islands but all the other neighbourhoods have somewhat blurred boundaries. The line between Vasastan and Norrmalm is a street, while Skeppsholmen is considered to be part of Djurgården even though it is connected to Norrmalm by a bridge but not to Djurgården. The Moderna Museet, which is on Skeppsholmen, is generally considered part of Djugården even though it is a five-minute walk from the entrance of the Nationalmuseum.

submitted to the academy for consideration of membership, but they also showcase exceptional work by international names. It's also got one of the largest collections of art by women because it was one of the first academies in Europe to accept women, even informally. This may not be everyone's cup of tea and it probably isn't for very young children, but it could give junior Picassos something to aspire to. If you have a few minutes to spare, it's a fun stop to add to your itinerary. Plus, it's free! The gallery only opens from 11am to 4pm, so if you're hoping to visit, squeeze it in between other activities. It is small though so it shouldn't take you more than 1½ to two hours to see everything properly.

In Their Footsteps WALKING TOUR

The **Stockholm Municipal Council** offers a set of curated and themed walking tours *(stadsmuseet.stockholm/en/group-booking/city-walks; group rate 3190kr)* that are booked directly with vetted and verified tour guides who have a passion for the city. In Norrmalm and the central Stockholm area, these tours cover some of the luminaries of Swedish design and manufacturing, whose lives would have intersected in this area as the city began to expand north. The short 90-minute tour is a great way to support a small local business and get the insights of a local who has spent time thinking about the best stories and tips to share with people who are limited on time. Book by email at boka.stadsmuseet@stockholm.se and ask about joining a group if travelling solo.

City of Culture FESTIVAL

Every summer, towards the end of August, the streets and spaces of Stockholm come alive with the **Kulturfestivalen** (*kulturfestivalen.stockholm.se; admission free*), the largest cultural festival in the country. The festival takes place over a one-week period and most of the venues are in Norrmalm, except the Skeppsbron in Gamla Stan and the Båtskenen boat party hosted on a boat docked off Gamla Stan. The festival programme is packed – it's almost as if the entire city gets in on this celebration of music, culture and dance. The programme goes up earlier in the year so if you have specific music and cultural tastes, plan early and create a schedule that allows you to walk between stages. Otherwise, if you happen to be in town during that week, you can just amble around between Norrmalm's main squares, from Sergels Tog all the way to Kungsträdgården and you'll get a little bit of the flavour of the city. And the best part is that it's all 100% free.

Small Space, Big Statement ART GALLERY

MAP: 11 P52 **E4**

Fans of small art venues will absolutely love the **Wetterling Gallery** *(wetterlinggallery.com; admission free)*. The private gallery is an eclectic collection of modern art that is fun and easy to experience, with regularly rotating exhibitions featuring emerging Swedish artists and established international names. If you find yourself in the Kungsträdgården and at a loose end, it's worth wandering inside to see the 'who's who' of up-and-coming Swedish artists. Entrance is free and the gallery is only moderately sized, so unless you plan to examine each of the paintings in great detail, this should be an hour or two of your time in Stockholm.

Ice, Ice Baby

BAR

MAP: 12 P52 **B4**

Should you go to the **Icebar** (p65) It depends. It is definitely a once-in-a-lifetime experience that has a unique vibe that will give you some great memories and photographs to look back on. Is it the best bar in Stockholm? Probably not. The novelty is nice and entertaining for what it is – a tourist attraction that draws a lot of people who want to be seen at the Icebar, rather than people who actually want to be at the Icebar. It's hard to enjoy your drink when you're cold no matter how many layers you have on or that they offer you, so a lot of people don't hang out at the bar for too long. That said, it makes a great photo op and a story about your time in Stockholm, and the drinks are good. Hundreds of thousands of people make the pilgrimage every year, so if you have great company and a high tolerance for cold, why not?

And All That Jazz

LIVE MUSIC

AT THE CENTRE OF IT ALL

T-Centralen is the main tunnelbana station in Stockholm and you'll probably go through here if you are connecting from the north to the south and vice versa. Because so many forms of transport go through here on different levels, it can be a little intimidating if you're in a hurry. There is signage everywhere but the easiest way to get your bearings it to pay attention to the terminal station for a sense of direction. And make time to visit the station on a day when you're not in a hurry. Look up and around – this is one of the most artistic stations in the city, including the abstract mosaics in the entrance hallways, the bird motifs on the commuter rail platforms and the artistic glory of the so-called 'blue platform'.

ART ON THE UNDERGROUND

Stockholm is incredibly proud of the art displayed in its tunnelbana (metro) stations, and three of the most interesting are found in Norrmalm within walking distance of Hötorget square. Hötorget station is one of the oldest tunnelbana stations, completed in 1952 and built in a classic brutalist fashion with its original square, powder-blue tiles evoking the halls of a mental institution in a film. This might not sound particularly good, but brutalism is back in a big way and the austere simplicity today feels artistic and kitschy, accentuated by the neon lights that were added in 1998.

MAP: 13 P52 **E2**

Stockholm loves jazz, and one of the great monuments to this love is the **Glenn Miller Café** on Brunnsgatan. This space sells itself as a music venue first with food and drinks coming in second, but it does both pretty well. Concerts take place every day except Sunday and usually feature Swedish acts, although international names in the genre sometimes drop by too. Three sets are performed each night and you can stay for one or pay for all three, but if you're not here for dinner you will have to stand at the bar. And if you just come for the bar, you will still have to buy a ticket for whatever performance is slated for the day. Weekends can be a little crowded and large groups must book in advance. This is also one of the flagship venues of the Stockholm Jazz Festival.

See p52 for map of locations

Best Places for...

€ Budget €€ Midrange €€€ Top End

Eating

Swedish Food

Hellbergs €€
See 6 C3
On lower level of Hötorghallen. Great for Swedish bites. *hellbergsfagelvilt.se; 10am-7pm Mon-Fri, 10am-4pm Sat*

Bakfickan €€€
14 F5
High-end take on Swedish classics. *operahuset.se/en/restauranger/bakfickan; 11:30am-11pm Mon-Fri, from noon Sat*

High-End Dining

Operakällaren €€€
15 F3
Award-winning fine dining within the Operan complex. *operahuset.se/en/lokaler/operakallaren; 6pm-1am Tue-Thu, noon-1am Fri & Sat*

Frantzén €€€
16 B3
Award-winning dining with a fixed tasting menu that takes all diners on a journey. It's small and fills up fast so book in advance. *restaurantfrantzen.com; 11am-1pm Mon-Fri*

Vegetarian

Holy Greens €
17 E4
Salads and veggies in the heart of Norrmalm. *8am-8pm Mon-Thu, to 7pm Fri, 11am-6pm Sat & Sun*

Underbar €€
18 B1
Lebanese food with plenty of options. *restaurangunderbar.se; 11am-2.30pm & 5pm to late Mon-Fri, 4pm to late Sat & Sun*

Mix & Match

K25 €
19 E2
Food hall with a bit of everything where you can pick up great meals to go. *k25.nu; 11am-9pm Mon-Sat*

Drinking

Eclectic Nights Out

Fasching
See 1 A3
Live music and dancing accompanied by drinks menu and food. *fasching.se; 11pm to late*

Café Opera
20 F5
Glitz and glamour for those looking for a high-end night out. *operahuset.se; 10am-3am Wed, Fri & Sat*

Icebar
See 12 B4
A once-in-a-lifetime experience if you can stand the cold. *icehotel.com/icebar-icehotel; 1-10.45pm Mon-Sun*

Shopping

Retail Therapy

NK
21 E4
Stockholm's largest department store offers a selection of local fashion, food and more. *10am-7pm Mon-Fri, to 6pm Sat, 11am-5pm Sun*

Mood Stockholm
22 E3
The best of Swedish food, design and fashion in an especially curated environment. *10am-7pm Mon-Fri, to 6pm Sat, 11am–5pm Sun*

See p84
for eating,
drinking and
shopping
listings

Explore Djurgården & Skeppsholmen

The green heart of Stockholm, Djurgården has lived many lives, including as a hunting ground for Swedish royals and a dock for the Swedish navy. Today it is one of Stockholm's most visited spaces with more museums and art galleries than you can count, an amusement park and kilometres of trails that offer some of the city's finest walking and cycling. Nearby Skeppsholmen is smaller but has had a similarly rich history, including as a major military station and today is home to some of Stockholm's most iconic museums. Don't skip the nearby Kastellholmen and its stunning views of the bay.

Getting Around

Bus

The 67 bus runs between Djurgården and Östermalm while the 69 bus connects Norrmalm to the island.

Tram

The 7 tram connects Djurgården to T-Centraalen in Norrmalm. On weekends or summer weekdays, the 7N heritage tram connects Norrmalmstorg and Waldemarsudde on

Boat

An SL card is valid on the Djurgårdsfärjan between Slussen and Djurgården via Skeppsholmen.

THE BEST

BIG MUSEUM
Nordiska Museet (p78)

SMALL MUSEUM
Prins Eugens Waldemarsudde (p83)

ART GALLERY
Thielska Galleriet (p80)

CAFE
Rosendals Trädgårdskafe (p84)

CHILDREN'S ATTRACTION
Junibacken (p80)

Skeppsholmen

Tram Line 7
Strandvägen
Styrmansgatan
Djurgårdsbron
Nobelgatan
Royal Djurgården Visitor Center
Djurgårdsbrunnsviken
Ladugårdslandsviken
Galärparken
Junibacken
Nordiska Museet
Nordiska Museet/ Vasamuseet
Galärvarvsvägen
Tyghusparken
Vasamuseet
Galärkyrkogården
Rosendalsvägen
De Besches Väg
Rosendals Slott
Stockholm Toy Museum
Slupskjulsvägen
Skeppsholmen
Spritmuseum
Hazeliusporten
Skansen
Sirishovsvägen
Rosendalsterrassen
Batteriparken
Moderna Museet
Viking Museum
Djurgårdsvägen
Orangerivägen
Djurgården
Excercisplan
Liljevalchs Konsthall
Solliddsbacken
DJURGÅRDEN
Valmundsvägen
Svensksundsparken
Långa Raden
Liljevalchs/Gröna Lund
ABBA: The Museum
Amiralitetsparken
Skansen Akvariet
Lilla Allmänna Gränd
Singelbacken
Bellmansro
Gröna Lund Tivoli
Tram Line 7
Djurgårdsvägen
Strömmen
Kastellparken
Kastellholmen
Djurgårdsslätten
Waldemarsudde
Prins Eugens Väg
Saltsjön
Beckholmen
Waldemarsviken
Prins Eugens Waldemarsudde
0 500 m
0 0.25 miles
For more see
Top Experiences p69
Experiences p78
Eating p84
Drinking p84
Shopping p85

★ TOP EXPERIENCE

Skansen

Wander through snapshots of life from the pre-Industrial era in Sweden and other Nordic countries at the world's largest open-air museum, curated to entertain and educate attendees of all ages.

A Walk Through Time

Skansen is designed and curated as an open-air museum. It's basically a small town and you could easily have a great day wandering through the grounds and experiencing the buildings and exhibitions on your own, enjoying traditional crafts, culture and foods. There are live demos during the day as well as restaurants and shops. It can be a bit overwhelming if you don't know where to start, so hop on an introductory tour, which is included in the admission price. The 30-minute tour in English gives you an overview of all the buildings on the grounds and their cultural significance, a general sense of the layout and an idea of how to orient your visit. The tour starts by the escalator hall and does not have to be prebooked, but it does only run once a day on weekdays and twice on the weekends, so plan your visit accordingly.

MAP P68 **D3**

PLANNING TIP
If you're planning to visit more than once, the annual pass is worth the investment as it costs less than two single day tickets.

Sing Your Heart Out

On eight Tuesdays during the summer, Skansen hosts concerts on the grounds that begin with massive sing-alongs and end in dance concerts that run until about 10pm. Wander through the museums during the day and then finish your evening

Check out the schedule of interactive events before you go.

KIRK FISHER/SHUTTERSTOCK ©

QUICK BREAK
Café Petissan (p84) on Storgatan is an excellent place to grab a *fika* (coffee and pastry) with a delightful ambience. Fresh pastries are served throughout the day.

outside, sitting on the grass watching the sun go down while surrounded by Swedes belting out Swedish folk songs and classics at full volume. This is an excellent, kid-friendly activity that can help the little ones – and the kids at heart – burn off excess energy during the longer summer days. The songs are in Swedish but the vibes transcend language, so gather your crew, grab a frosty drink and soak up the energy.

Winter Delights

Sweden's long, cold winter nights can be intimidating for people who are new to them but there is always something to do at Skansen, even in the heart of winter. The Christmas market here is particularly charming, as is the folk tradition of Lucia – a distinctly Swedish celebration of the end of autumn and the hope of new light for the winter – commemorating the martydom of a Swedish saint of the same name. A particular highlight of the deep winter is the 6 February celebration of the Sami National Day. In 1992 the Sami, northern Sweden's indigenous people, came together on this day to organise for more rights and protections from the government, and since then, the day is commemorated throughout the country. At Skansen, this involves a week of music, dance and food, as well as showcasing the Sami holdings in the museum's collections. The Swedes say that there's no such thing as bad weather, only bad gear, so throw on your thickest coat and join in the celebrations.

For the Little Ones

Skansen is one of the most kid-friendly places in Stockholm, which is a very high bar in a city where museums and other sites go to great lengths to include children. Lill Skansen is a particularly huge draw for younger visitors because they not only get to see animals you would a traditional zoo, but if your little one is particularly keen on animals, you can book them a 'mini zookeeper' experience where they get to work with one of the zookeepers for 1½ hours to showcase an animal to other young visitors that day (900kr, email bokning@skansen.se to reserve). The experience requires at least two children aged between four and 10 to run, and the cost of the ticket includes entry for one adult.

SERVICE ANIMALS WELCOME

Pets are not allowed at Skansen because many of the installations feature animals that could get sick if they are exposed to illness. Service animals are exempted but they must be easily identifiable by their harnesses and owners must sign a declaration at the entrance that they have no infectious diseases.

★ TOP EXPERIENCE

Vasamuseet

For centuries, people have left here on ships to explore the world. Bask in Sweden's long maritime history at Scandinavia's most-visited **museum** that is a shrine to both the scale and the limits of the ambitions of this sea-faring nation.

MAP P68 **B2**

PLANNING TIP
Tours in English leave every 30 minutes and are included in the price of admission.

Scan this QR code for combination tickets, which include the Museum of Wrecks.

The Vasa

For centuries the inhabitants of Sweden and the greater Nordic region have built mighty ships that have left this cold corner of the world and wandered in search of all manner of treasures. One of the finest specimens of these vessels is the *Vasa*, at once representing the ambition and the failure of Sweden's sea-faring prowess. This towering example is the centrepiece of the museum, immaculately preserved in the cavernous heart of the building through many phases after its ill-fated maiden voyage in 1628. You can learn more about the *Vasa*'s history by taking a self-guided tour of the museum, but a 25-minute guided tour is included in the price of admission and is accompanied by such rich storytelling that you would be cheating yourself if you skipped it. Meet your guide at the entrance of the museum on the hour and at the half-hour mark from 10.30am until closing.

Ahoy Mateys!

The Vasamuseet is also a monument to Swedish naval history, particularly King Gustav II Adolf who commissioned the *Vasa* in order to make a point about his own military prowess and to poke fun at his enemies. The elaborate sculptures carved into the ship's sides and interiors are not just ornaments: they are part of the king's message to the world about Sweden's military strength. The Vasa Up Close exhibition allows you to get closer to these fascinating details that are also a

BUMBLE DEE/SHUTTERSTOCK ©

testament to the craftsmanship of the day. Some of the replicas are painted in the original colours of the *Vasa* and this also increases your ability to imagine the ship as it was in its prime.

Family Fun

If you decide not to take the guided tour, or if you want to stay a bit longer at the Vasamuseeet and enjoy some quality time with your family, you can always take the family trail. This is a map that is curated to guide visitors through the museum with stops that showcase the most fascinating parts of the ship. The experience is particularly designed with children in mind and is more of a treasure hunt than it is an in-depth exploration of naval or preservation history. Get your free copy of the map at the visitor deck or print out one in advance from the Vasamuseet website (*vasamuseet.se*).

★ TOP EXPERIENCE

Moderna Museet

No other museum in Stockholm quite matches the contemporary vibe of the city as much as the **Moderna Museet**. Sure there are some big names here, but this is a space for enthusiasts who can appreciate excellent modern art without name-dropping.

MAP P68 **A2**

PLANNING TIP
The easiest way to get to the museum is to walk onto Skeppsholmen from Kungsträdgården in Norrmalm, which takes about 10 minutes, but you can also walk comfortably from Gamla Stan.

Download free audio guides for exhibitions on your phone before you arrive.

The Collection

The heart of the Moderna Museet is the collection that features both world-renowned artists like Andy Warhol and Swedish names that have shaped the country's art world. Up on the 4th floor (which is actually the ground floor at street level) spread across three rooms, this collection comprises contemporary European art. But rather than following a chronological order, the museum pulls from its vast holdings and displays rotating exhibitions around specific themes. The collection is large and still growing so there's a near-endless stream of stories that can be told, making this one of the highlights of living in Stockholm, let alone visiting it.

Study Gallery

One of the most interesting innovations at the Moderna Museet is the Study Gallery, a space on the 2nd floor that allows you to experience the museum's collection without wandering around. The idea was conceived in the 1960s but it wasn't realised until 2008, and today it feels like what a museum would be like if it was designed by The Jetsons, as 30 screens focused on specific themes descend to eye level and you get to stand still and have the museum come to you.

RITU MANOJ JETHANI/SHUTTERSTOCK ©

Art for the People

The Moderna Museet also showcases a significant collection of sculptures in its sculpture garden around Skeppsholmen. Some of the art is a little more obvious than others – *The Four Elements* installation, for example, is very difficult to confuse with anything else other than a form of artistic expression. But some of it is more subtle, like the grassy knoll that you will pass if you circumnavigate the perimeter of the island. This unassuming tiny hill is actually an installation called *Louisa* that the artist Thomas Woodruff installed in 1988 and is intentionally dynamic, changing with the seasons and with time. An audio guide to the sculptures on the island is available on the museum website *(modernamuseet.se)* and at the visitor entrance.

QUICK BREAK

The cafe and restaurant at the Moderna Museet offer excellent views over the water, particularly in the summer. They also regularly connect the specials to exhibition themes.

WALKING TOUR

Djurgården Sculpture Walk

Djurgården feels like an enormous park. The island was once a royal hunting ground and then a holiday residence, and it still retains its garden-like feel, but with many secret treasures between the grassy knolls and along its shores. This walk seeks out some of the sculptures dotted across the park.

START	END	LENGTH
Blå Porten	Gravitational Ripples	4km; one to two hours

1 Blå Porten

The **Blå Porten** (Blue Gate) was the entrance to Djurgården for non-royal visitors and is the first point of access for anyone arriving at Djurgården on foot. At the Royal Visitor Center nearby you can rent traditional Dutch bikes that you can use to cycle around the island.

2 Life Rings

Follow Djurgårdsbrunnsviken, the channel that separates from Ladugårdsgärdet to the north, until you arrive at the *Life Rings* sculpture, a complex tower of white- and red-striped lifebuoys, one of the many sculptures in the park that are part of the Princess Estelle Sculpture Park.

3 Hoop-La

As you walk past the Rosendals Slott (a small palace built for Karl XIV Johan in the 1820s, and an early example of a prefabricated house) and beside the footbridge across to Ladugårdsgärdet, you'll find the dynamic aluminium and steel sculpture *Hoop-La* by Alice Aycock.

4 Wind Sculpture

Walk up the wooded hill to the south to find Yinka Shonibare's *Wind Sculpture*, a remarkable piece that pulls off the trick of making bronze seem like a billowing batik print fabric. This is a good place for a short break at a nearby cafe.

5 Untold

Follow Rosendalsvägen back towards the water and you'll come to Charlotte Gyllenhamar's *Untold*, a tall bronze sculpture that resembles a human form standing sentry over the beech grove close to Rosendal's Slott.

6 Inner Flow of Life

If you get on Israel-af-Ströms väg, or just generally walk with the Rosendals Slott behind you, you'll come to the latest sculpture acquired for the sculpture park – *Inner Flow of Life* by Guiseppe Penone, which looks like a small tree growing out the hard rock.

7 Gustaf Frödings Skulptur

Continue towards Djurgårdsbron to find this 1921 sculpture of the Swedish poet looking towards his final home. While here, listen and look out for the abundant birdlife nearby, including tawny owls that nest nearby.

8 Gravitational Ripples

Walk towards the Thielska Gallereit on the far end of the island by following Manilavägen onto Djurgårdsvägen and you'll come to *Gravitational Ripples*, a memorial to the victims of the 2004 tsunami and a great place to rest your feet after your walk.

EXPERIENCES

A Taste of Nordic Life MUSEUMS

MAP: 1 P68 C2

You're in Stockholm for the first time, you're on a tight schedule and you want to go back home with a taste of what exactly makes Scandinavia unique to the rest of Europe. If this is you, do yourself a favour and head straight to the **Nordiska Museet** (*nordiska museet.se; adult/child 170kr/free*). This imposing building right at the entrance of Djurgården with its neo-Gothic architecture can be quite imposing, but it actually has several options for self-guided or guided tours that can be whittled down to as little as 45 minutes. Head straight to the top floor for the Nordic Life permanent exhibition for a quick cultural and historical tour, but if you can make a little more time, tag on the Arctic Life exhibition where you can learn more about Sami culture and walk through a room that has been designed to feel like a real iceberg.

Beyond the Beards & Boats MUSEUM

MAP: 2 P68 C2

What on earth is a Viking anyway? Find the answer to this and many other questions about the people who made up arguably Sweden's best-known historical time period at the **Viking Museum** (*the vikingmuseum.com; adult/child/under-6s 199kr/149kr/free*). There's beards and boats galore, but also a lot of insight into the women and children who stayed behind after the boats left, carving a life in sometimes hostile weather and difficult environments. Don't skip Rangfrid's Saga either. This 11-minute ride takes you through the experience of a Viking raid in Europe via the story of a single Viking – the cost is included in the price of the ticket. With the indefinite closure of the Medieval Museum, this is the best place in Stockholm to get closer to this slice of European history.

Under the Sea AQUARIUM

MAP: 3 P68 D3

If there are younger travellers in your group, the **Skansen Akvariet** (*skansen.se/aquarium; adult/child 160/80kr*) is a great place to spend a few hours burning off excess energy while learning. The 'aquarium' is a bit of a misnomer – it's actually more like a zoo featuring all kinds of animals, from those that live under the sea to those that don't. Much of the experience is interactive, including the manta ray tank. Adults may benefit from the clap-and-hug corner that happens on weekends during the high season. It's a very cool part of the aquarium where zookeepers create a safe environment to work with visitors to help them overcome their fear of spiders, snakes or birds. Entry to the aquarium is separate to entry to Skansen more generally, and it takes at least two hours to experience it fully, up to six hours if you're here to overcome your fear of arachnids.

Take a Ch-Ch-Chance on Me

MUSEUM

MAP: 4 P68 **C3**

The year is 1974. Afros, platforms and flared trousers are in, and at the Eurovision Song Contest in Brighton, a Swedish quartet is about to enter the history books with a catchy number that even 50 years later everyone will know the words to but never fully understand. This is ABBA's origin story – the band that forever changed pop music and whose lyrics and arrangements continue to enchant millions around the world. At **ABBA: The Museum** (*abbathemuseum.com; adult/child 239/100kr*) you can learn more about the making of the band and their legacy, but also hop into an interactive exhibit where you get to be the fifth member of the band. For an extra fee, you can go on the ABBA Djurgården tour that takes you to spots around the island where the band was photographed. Tickets are only sold online in advance and by time slot, so plan ahead.

First of a Kind

HISTORICAL HOME

MAP: 5 P68 **F2**

Away from the hubbub of Djurgården's other museums and nestled in a grove of carefully tended gardens is a house that isn't as impressive as Sweden's other royal homes, but tells an interesting story about how construction has evolved over time. **Rosendals Slott** (*kungligaslotten.se/english/royal-palaces-and-sites/rosendal-palace.html; adult/child 130/65kr*) was a summer home for Swedish royals built in a uniquely Swedish style and at least partially prefabricated. The interior of the palace remains largely unchanged including the furnishings and decor, so it feels like peering into the private lives of Swedish royals who came here specifically to hide away from us mere mortals. The palace was closed for guided tours at the time of writing, but you can still come here and wander around. Note that the park is closed in the winter except for prebooked group tours.

ROYAL NATIONAL CITY PARK

Djurgården and the adjacent parts of Östermalm form part of the Royal National City Park, an expansive stretch of green that runs all the way to Ulriksdal near Hagaparken. It is this park that gives Stockholm its open feel; a city hemmed in by nature rather than by tall buildings. Unlike many other large cities, the park is not entirely fenced in and, in fact, there are several homes in areas where you might expect residential and commercial activities to be excluded. It's a bit long for a single day's walk but if you're on an active holiday, it's a great place to cycle or run.

Small, But Mighty

GALLERY

MAP: 6 P68 **F3**

Edward Thiel built a home that was specially designed to accommodate his art collection and his desire to live amongst art. Although he had to sell the property to the Swedish government to recover from some bad financial decisions, the government kept the **Thielska Galleriet** (*thielskagalleriet.se; adult/child 150kr/free*) more or less intact, including furnishings, so you can pretend for an afternoon that you are also the grand patron of this stunning home and collection. The heart of the collection is held in two gallery rooms, but there's also a room dedicated to Norwegian painter Edvard Munch, one of Thiel's artistic friends. The gallery only opens in the afternoon on Tuesday to Sunday so don't plan a morning visit.

All Aboard!

CHILDREN'S ACTIVITY

MAP: 7 P68 **B1**

Do you remember the first book that you read that got you excited about reading? For millions of readers around the world Astrid Lindgren's **Pippi Longstocking** would be that book, and **Junibacken** (*junibacken.se; adult/child 165-225/160-190kr*) is a celebration of her works and other celebrated authors' books. The decibels at this cultural centre can be a little intimidating for older visitors, but focus on the fact that there's something truly special about a cultural space dedicated to reading, play and being young at heart. Kids will love the Story Train, a 15-minute ride through the museum's retelling of Lindgren's story of the same name – your entrance ticket contains a single free ticket. It also hosts the largest children's bookshop in Sweden so you can get some souvenirs for your young ones. Book tickets online in advance as prices vary and are sold in time slots.

FREE CHILDREN GO FREE

Stockholm is easily one of the most child-friendly cities in the world, with museums and other spaces offering free admission, as well as specially curated activities and installations for children. The problem is that 'child' is defined very differently between institutions. At some places, a child is anyone under 18, at others it's under 20, and for others still, teenagers might be required to pay a concessionary fee. Regardless, when visiting an attraction or purchasing a ticket – including transport tickets – it's worth asking if they offer special concessionary prices for children, seniors, students and visitors with disabilities as they usually do.

ACCESSIBILITY AT DJURGÅRDEN

The attractions on the islands of Djurgården and Skeppsholmen have varying levels of accessibility for people with disabilities and those requiring special support. As a general rule of thumb, museums will have the most accommodations while attractions like Grona Lund Tivoli may require a little planning to navigate. A note on Skansen (p69) – this is a large open-air museum that is essentially a small town, in a somewhat hilly part of the island. While wheelchairs can navigate most spaces, it may get tiring in a manual wheelchair; an electric one is recommended.

Chasing Thrills — AMUSEMENT PARK

MAP: 8 P68 C3

Spending your free time chasing death by defying heights and speed in an amusement park is admittedly not for everyone. **Gröna Lund Tivoli** (*gronalund.com; 420kr for a summer pass*) is immensely popular with local tourists because it is the only amusement park of its kind in Sweden and the rides are up to international standards. If you have a limited amount of time in Stockholm, this may not be a high priority because it's not a uniquely Swedish experience. But if you've never been to an amusement park it is certainly a great option and with only a limited number of rides, it shouldn't take more than an afternoon to catch the thrills you're chasing here. They are closed in the winter and some rides are age-restricted, so it may not be the best place for groups with very young children.

Getting Hot in Here — ACTIVITY

One of the most popular activities at Skansen (p69) is the glass-blowing workshop hosted by **Stockholms Glasbruk** (*stockholmsglasbruk.com; freeform workshop/groups of 6 1900/550kr*), close to the Hasselbacken hotel. The glassblowers here are keeping alive historical methods of glass-blowing and you're invited to make something such as a Christmas ornament or a small bowl that you can take home with you. The freeform workshop takes about an hour, and you get to pick the object that you want to make and then collect it later. A minimum of two adults are required for the freeform workshop. This is a very popular activity – they release slots at the beginning of the month and once they're gone, they're gone.

If You Build It... — MUSEUM

MAP: 9 P68 C2

One word that you will hear a lot used to discuss Sweden's relationship with alcohol is 'complicated'.

ON YOUR PHONE

Several of the museums in Stockholm allow you to download audio guides for free in advance, so if you're curating a trip before you arrive, this is one way that you can save time. Unfortunately it does involve downloading multiple apps. One particularly useful app is the free Kungliga promenader for a guided tour of the sculptures in the park, some of which are narrated by the artists who made the sculpture or installation.

Sweden has a long history of alcoholism that has led to unique developments like the Systembolaget approach where any drink with over 3.5% alcohol content can only be purchased at state-owned retailers. The **Spritmuseum** (*spiritmuseum.se; adult/child 190/95kr*) is a monument to this complication. It's more of a museum than other alcohol-based museums in the world that may focus only on celebrating brands – this takes a more critical approach, celebrating the art of making alcohol and the harms of abusing it. It is also home to the Absolut art collection, one of the largest collections of pop art in the world. It features several Warhol originals that are frequently featured in rotating exhibitions.

Try Something Different MUSEUM

MAP: **10** P68 C2

Big museums may not be your thing, and that's okay. Drop by the **Liljevalchs Konsthall** (*liljevalchs.se; adult/child 150kr/free*) instead. This relatively small gallery space hides between ABBA: The Museum (p79) and the Nordiska Museet, and sometimes doesn't get the love it deserves. But it is home to an amazing collection of contemporary Swedish art and design, and every year it hosts a spring showcase that celebrates the newest entries into the space. The iconic **Blå Porten Café** (p84), with it's celebrated vegetarian menu is also right by the entrance so you could combine a delicious lunch with a quick wander through the museum to burn it off.

Out on the Water BOATING

MAP: **11** P68 C1

You can't beat the sensation of being out on the water in Stockholm on a hot summer's day, and Djurgården is an excellent place to get your fix. Enquire about renting a kayak or a paddle boat to tour around the water from the **Royal Visitor Center**. The amphibious Ocean Bus also passes through the waterways and is a fun activity for families, especially when it makes that giant splash into the water. If your budget is tight, you can also use your SL card to get a self-curated tour of the islands – boats to Slussen leave from just outside the Thielska Galleriet and you can island-hop between Stockholm's inner islands this way.

Play On!

MUSEUM

MAP: 12 P68 **A2**

They say that if you want to grow old, stop playing, so if you're trying to avoid getting old, visit the **Stockholm Toy Museum** (*toy museum.se; adult/child 175/115kr*). If you're travelling with children this is a great card to have up your sleeve. The installations feature thousands of toys from around the world and even though they're not all especially Swedish, they are nostalgic for adults from all corners. The real advantage though is the special events that they host in the summer, which are some of the most interactive activities for kids and young adults. If you are short on time you could probably give it a miss, but if you're looking for a quirky place to spend an hour or two, and a cafe with an incredible view of the bay, it's worth your time.

Lunch with a View

MUSEUM

MAP: 13 P68 **E4**

has been home to some of the wealthiest people in Stockholm for so long, so it therefore makes sense that you'll find a few stately homes that have been turned into museums or otherwise preserved here. A small tour of these homes could involve Thielska Galleriet, Villa Lusthulsporten and **Prins Eugens Waldemarsudde** (*waldemarsudde.se; adult/child 170kr/free*). This latter museum is celebrated as the most beautiful in Stockholm for its wonderful interiors and delightful gardens. But its real secret is the restaurant on the grounds overlooking the open water, which serves a wonderful menu. On a summer day it can be hard to get a seat as the ferry to the island stops quite close by, but if you make it to the far side of the island, grab a rest and a fizzy drink here.

WEAR COMFORTABLE SHOES

Djurgården is a decently sized island and the paths are not exactly straightforward – several are pedestrian- and cyclist-only so they may not be the easiest to find. You're more likely to get lost on the eastern side of the island than the west because there is more greenery and fewer signposted buildings. If you're pressed for time, stick to the perimeter of the island, which will take longer and involve a mix of surfaced roads and unpaved paths, but will eventually lead you back to Blå Porten.

LISTINGS

Best Places for...

See p68 for map of locations

€ Budget €€ Midrange €€€ Top End

Eating

Fika & Pastries

Blå Porten Café €€

14 C3

Lovely cafe with a beautiful garden and extensive vegetarian options. *blaporten.com; 11am-8pm Wed & Fri-Mon, to 9pm Tue & Thu*

Skroten Cafe €€

15 C3

Excellent food in a rustic setting with unfinished tables and mismatched furniture, but it remains busy for a reason. *skrotens.se; 11am-4pm Mon-Fri, to 5pm Sat & Sun*

Café Petissan €€

16 C2

Authentic Swedish *fika* served in an authentic 18th-century house. *cafepetissan.com; 11am-3pm Mon-Fri, to 4pm Sat & Sun*

Award-Winning Dining

Lilla Hasslebacken €€

17 C3

Quaint and charming lunch cafe with plenty of Swedish offerings. *lillahasselbacken.se; 10am-3pm*

Rosendals Trädgårdskafe €€

18 E2

Farm-to-table organic menu with a wonderful bakery nearby. It smells like fresh bread and happiness here. *rosendalstradgard.se/tradgardskafe; 10am-4pm*

Aira €€€

19 F4

The award-winning tasting menus and stunning views are worth the trek across the island. Reserve ahead as it gets busy. *aira.se; 6-11pm Tue & Wed, from noon Thu-Sat*

Drinking

Get in the Spirit

Spritmuseum

See 9 C2

Yes, it's a museum, but the staff actually make great cocktails and they also organise tastings. *spiritmuseum.se; 11am-7pm Sun-Tue, to 10pm Wed-Sat*

Hotel Hasselbacken

20 C2

This is the hotel bar but it does serve drinks and has long opening hours so is a great way to wind down after a tour. *hasselbacken.com; 11.30am-midnight Mon-Fri*

Djurgårdsbron

21 B1

Live music and drinks in a place at the edge of the island that's popular with locals and tourists alike. *sjocafeet.se; 9am-7pm, to sunset in the summer*

DOTMILLER1986/SHUTTERSTOCK ©

Shopping

Museum Shopping

Skansen

22 C3

The museum shop at Skansen is an excellent place to pick up hand-crafted souvenirs and they also produce their own range of keep-sakes and home goods. *skansen.se; hours vary*

ABBA: The Museum

See 4 C3

All the band-themed paraphernalia that your heart could desire is found in the museum gift shop, including replicas of iconic outfits (pictured). *abbathemuseum.com; 10am-6pm Fri-Wed, to 8pm Thu*

Junibacken

See 7 B1

The largest children's bookshop in Stockholm has a significant selection in English as well as games. *junibacken.se; 10am-5pm Sun-Fri, from 9am Sat*

See p99
for eating, drinking and shopping listings

Explore Södermalm

Known locally as 'Soder', Södermalm is home to some of the city's coolest neighbourhoods. Long a working-class neighbourhood, it's now decidedly gentrified – a sleepy island where middle-class Stockholmer's enjoy the Scandinavian cool that the country is known for. Even so, Södermalm is dotted with independent fashion boutiques and design stores, vintage sellers, cafes, bars and music venues. Whatever your price point, there's sure to be something that captures either the Swedish classics or nouveau trends that are taking the world by storm. Södermalm is also home to some of Stockholm's most iconic outdoor spaces, including parks, urban beaches and panoramic viewpoints. This is a great place to unwind and to pick up souvenirs, or to experience local life away from the crowds.

Getting Around

Bus

Slussen is the main bus stop in southern Stockholm and you can walk to many of the attractions from here, although you do need to ascend several stairs or hills. Wheelchair users may prefer connecting to other bus lines.

Tram

Stockholm's Sodra station gets you right into the centre of Södermalm and is within walking distance of Mariatorget station.

Boat

Ferries to other parts of Stockholm and the archipelago depart from and return to Slussen regularly. SL cards are valid for trips within central Stockholm.

★

THE BEST

VIEWPOINT
Monteliusvägen (p93)

URBAN BEACH
Tanto Strandbad (p93)

MUSEUM
Fotografiska (p90)

SWEDISH RESTAURANT
Pelikan (p96)

SECOND-HAND SHOPPING
Judits (p99)

Södermalm

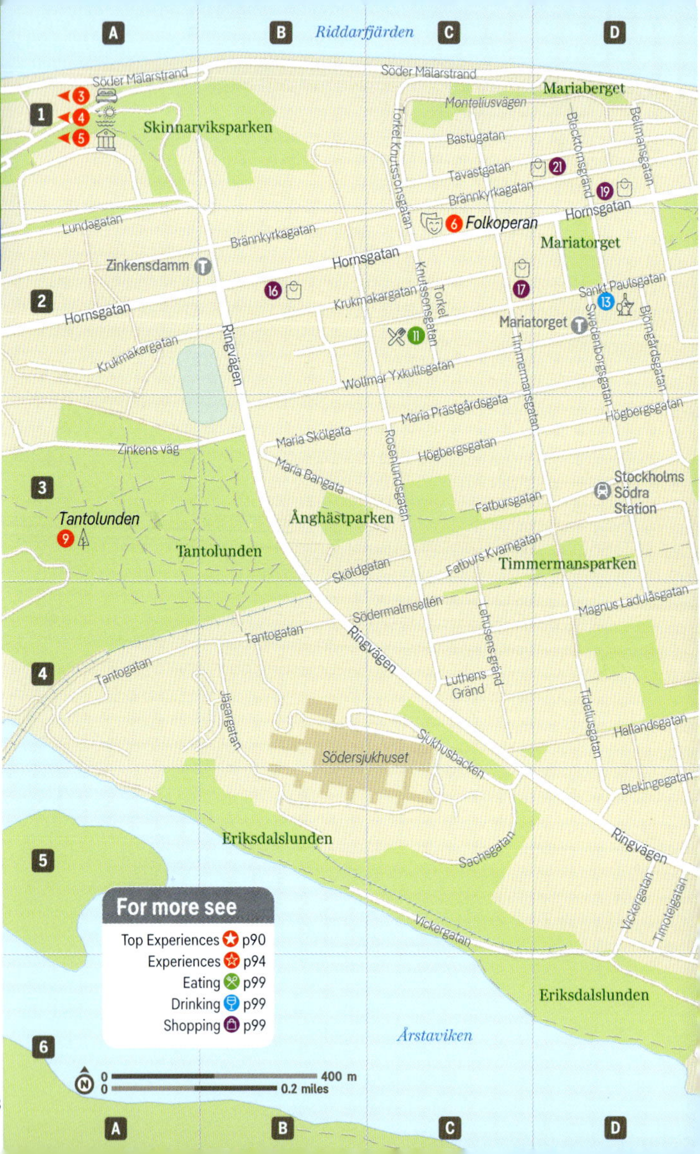
Riddarfjärden
Söder Mälarstrand
Skinnarviksparken
Mariaberget
Monteliusvägen
Bastugatan
Tavastgatan
Brännkyrkagatan
Hornsgatan
Torkel Knutssonsgatan
Bellmansgatan
Blecktornsgränd
Folkoperan
Mariatorget
Lundagatan
Zinkensdamm
Krukmakargatan
Sankt Paulsgatan
Swedenborgsgatan
Björngårdsgatan
Timmermansgatan
Ringvägen
Wollmar Yxkullsgatan
Maria Prästgårdsgata
Högbergsgatan
Maria Skölgata
Maria Bangata
Zinkens väg
Rosenlundsgatan
Stockholms Södra Station
Fatbursgatan
Tantolunden
Ånghästparken
Fatburs Kvarngata
Timmermansparken
Sköldgatan
Södermalmsallén
Magnus Ladulåsgatan
Tantogatan
Lehusens gränd
Luthens Gränd
Tideliusgatan
Jägargatan
Hallandsgatan
Södersjukhuset
Sjukhusbacken
Blekingegatan
Eriksdalslunden
Sachsgatan
Vickergatan
Timotejgatan
Årstaviken
For more see
Top Experiences p90
Experiences p94
Eating p99
Drinking p99
Shopping p99
400 m
0.2 miles

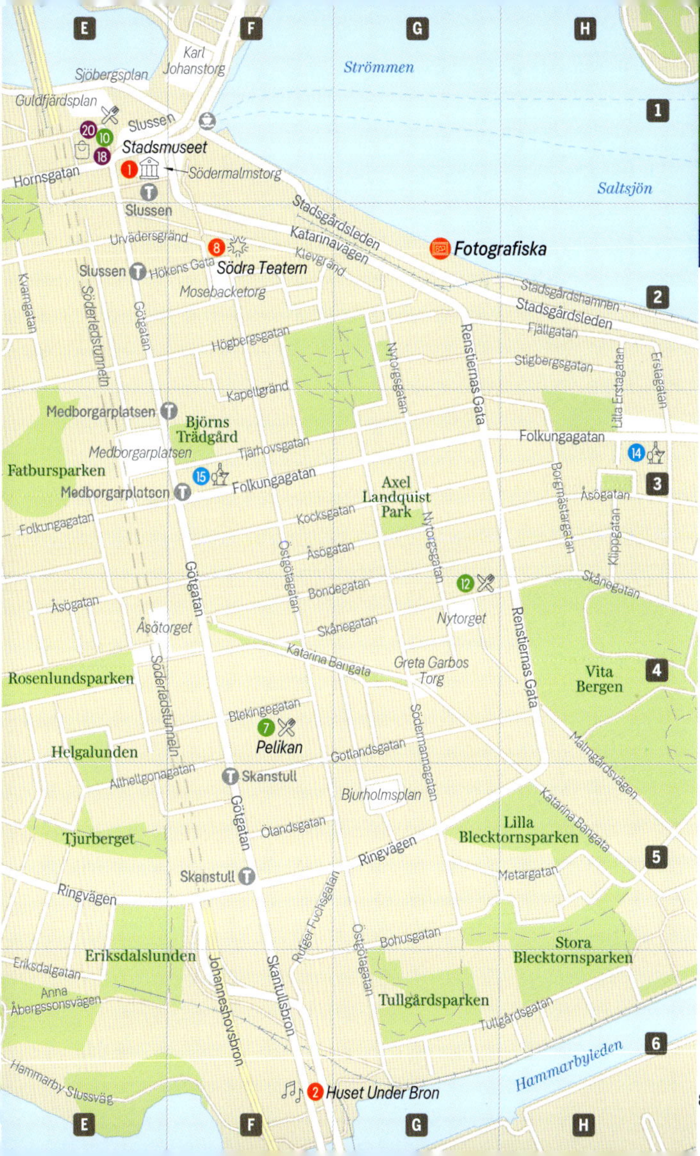

Strömmen
Saltsjön
Slussen
Stadsmuseet
Södermalmstorg
Fotografiska
Södra Teatern
Björns Trädgård
Medborgarplatsen
Fatbursparken
Axel Landquist Park
Nytorget
Greta Garbos Torg
Vita Bergen
Rosenlundsparken
Pelikan
Helgalunden
Skanstull
Bjurholmsplan
Lilla Blecktornsparken
Tjurberget
Ringvägen
Eriksdalslunden
Stora Blecktornsparken
Tullgårdsparken
Hammarbyleden
Huset Under Bron
Hornsgatan
Götgatan
Folkungagatan
Renstiernas Gata
Katarina Bangata
Johanneshovsbron
Skanstullsbron

★ TOP EXPERIENCE

Fotografiska

One of the largest museums in the world dedicated exclusively to photography, **Fotografiska** features the museum's own collection alongside a regularly rotating showcase of internationally renowned artists. But even if photographs are not your thing, this is a great location with excellent views to grab a meal and sundowner drinks.

MAP P89 **G2**

PLANNING TIP
The museum restaurants are incredibly popular and if it's an important part of your itinerary, do reserve in advance.

Scan this QR code to prebook your ticket and save.

The Collection

If you're after a more relaxed museum experience, the excellent exhibitions and installations at Fotografiska will delight you. This excellently curated contemporary museum is dedicated to photography in the most expansive sense of the word, and features collections from internationally renowned artists. They also have a permanent collection that rotates through the various galleries.

Unless you're a keen expert in photography, the visit shouldn't take more than a few hours, and then you can enjoy the excellent location of the building itself. Fotografiska is hosted in one of the coolest locations in Stockholm, in a renovated customs hall on the north bank of Södermalm. The red-brick building was designed by the architect Ferdinand Boberg and completed in 1906. It offers unparalleled views of the straits between the islands.

The Bistro

At the entrance of Fotografiska is the Bistro, a more casual dining experience that is popular with locals for after-work drinks because it overlooks the water and the food is immaculate. More hearty snacks than full meals, the Bistro is a great place to finish off a day of walking. But if you're planning to do that, book a table before you enter the museum

RADIOKAFKA/SHUTTERSTOCK ©

so that it will be ready by the time you are done – it can take a while for a table to free up.

The Restaurant

Fotografiska's rooftop restaurant underwent a major renovation in 2024 and reopened to high praise. The menu is inspired by local cuisine but it's nothing like what you'll find elsewhere – experimental and seasonal, and always with an eye towards the environment and sustainability. Plus you can eat while enjoying one of the best views in Stockholm looking over at Gamla Stan and Djurgarden. It's a set menu with recommended pairings and your payment includes entry to the exhibitions at the museum. On weekends they serve an excellent brunch with pastries. Book early – it fills up fast.

WALKING TOUR

Södermalm

Södermalm is primarily a residential area with the majority of the attractions concentrated in the northern part of the island. Walking between Fotografiska and Tantolunden will give you a great sense of orientation and key landmarks. This might be a little challenging so wear good shoes and take your time!

START	END	LENGTH
Fotografiska	Tanto Strandbad	6km; two to three hours

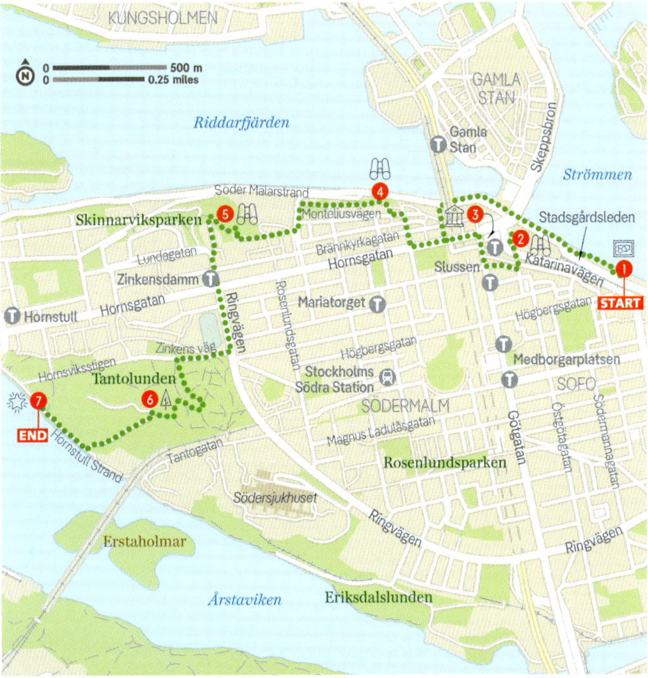

1 Fotografiska

Aside from the contents of the museum, the **Fotografiska** (p90) building is also an architecturally significant monument in Stockholm.

2 Katerinahissen

Walk towards Slussen and the Gondolen exit at the tunnelbana (metro) station for the **Katarinahissen** lift. The lift is not operational while construction of New Slussen (p97) continues, but if you can manage the stairs, you can get to the top for panoramic views of the city.

3 Stadsmuseet

A five-minute walk from Katarinahissen on Rysgården is the **Stadsmuseet** (p94), a free museum celebrating the heritage of the city. It's a bit tricky to get between the locations because it involves a winding descent – the least confusing option is to walk back towards Götgatan.

4 Mariaberget

Just around the corner is Hornsgatan, Södermalm's second main street and the location of its many shops and restaurants. Off the junction with Bellmansgatan is the road towards **Mariaberget**, another viewpoint with stunning views over Kungsholmen and the Stadshuset. The walkway that winds through the park is Monteliusvägen, offering the best views of Kungsholmen.

5 Skinnarviksberget

With the open waters of Lake Mälaren on your right and Slussen behind you, walking along any of the main roads will lead you to **Skinnarviksberget**, another iconic viewpoint and one of the highest points in Stockholm.

6 Tantolunden

Meander slowly back to Honsgatan and walk with Slussen behind you and Lake Mälaren on your right towards the edge of the island. On the left, somewhat underneath the large interchange is an entry point to **Tantolunden** (p97), the largest park in Södermalm.

7 Tanto Strandbad

In the summer, the water's edge at Tantolunden turns into one of the most popular hotspots in Stockholm, with people gathering to enjoy a sunny day out. It's not a beach in the traditional sense of the word as there's no sand, but Tanto Strandbad does get plenty of sun, which is very much appreciated on long summer days.

EXPERIENCES

Delve into the City's Past

MUSEUM

MAP: 1 P88 E1

The **Stadsmuseet** *(stadsmuseet.stockholm)* is a dynamic collection that documents the history of the city through the experiences of real individuals who have lived or worked there. The museum is housed in a 1680 building designed by Nicodemus Tessin the Elder, one of Sweden's most important architects. The displays are engaging and very creative, and many are also hands-on so that people of all age groups can get involved through costumes and play. A number of events are also available in English to allow visitors to participate. Perhaps most importantly, the museum is free, so if you're visiting Stockholm on a budget, it's a great way to get your culture and history fix without breaking the bank.

Pro tip: the museum also offers a themed map of the city based on popular books or films so you can curate a self-guided tour based on your own interests!

Party with the Locals

ENTERTAINMENT VENUE

MAP: 2 P88 F6

Sometimes you just want to go somewhere and get everything you need to have a good time. **Huset Under Bron** *(husetunderbron.se)* is this kind of entertainment complex under the Skanstull bridge in Södermalm. Head here to sample the flavourful plant-based cuisine at Växthuset – order the seven-course menu as most of the inventive dishes are small. On Fridays and Saturdays dance the night away at a couple of bars and clubs, including the Red Room (which is actually decorated pink). From May to September it all morphs into an outdoor party space. This ultra-popular club has a full-on festival atmosphere with everything from table tennis and video games to street food, live music and pumping DJs.

Life at the Fringe

FESTIVAL

MAP: 3 P88 A1

Reimersholmen is a small island attached so well to Södermalm that you might not even notice you're on a separate island. Although predominantly residential, it's worth knowing about as this is a location of one of Stockholm's most enjoyable festivals, the **Stockholm Fringe Festival** (*stockholmfringe.com*). Modelled on the Edinburgh Fringe Festival, in late August this festival celebrates live theatre and comedy shows. At the Reimersholme Hotel you don't just get accommodation – this is also a live music venue that offers a variety of activities including table tennis tables and an outdoor beer garden. In the summer months it's a great place to meet friends and sip beers and wine with the locals.

Island Life

BEACH

MAP: 4 P88 A1

Connected to Södermalm by bridges are two of Stockholm's smaller islands: **Långholmen** and **Reimmersholmen**. Långholmen is immensely popular with locals for picnics, walks and after-work swims. There are two options for swimming – one is the Långholmsbadet with its calm, crisp waters and beautiful views. The swimming area is small but it's enough for anyone who's just looking to cool off as opposed to working out. The second option is Långholmens Klippbad but note there are no facilities here – bring everything you need, including a card or some change to pay for the changing room if you're not comfortable changing in front of others.

I'm on a Boat!

KAYAKING

Some people just need to keep busy, even while on holiday, and kayaking can be a great compromise activity for those that who need to move and those who are happy to lay back and let someone else do the paddling. Rent a kayak from **Långholmen Kayak** (*langholmenkajak.se/*) and either take an independent paddle around the island or a guided tour led by one of the team. The circuit isn't long but it is very pleasant and completely accessible to beginners after a brief introduction from the team.

Blast from the Past

MUSEUM

MAP: 5 P88 A1

Långholmen is a great place to imagine what Stockholm was like in the past. There's the small **Långholmen Prison Museum** (*langholmen.com/en/experience/prison-museum*) at the Långholmen hotel, and a cafe where you can sip a quiet coffee or read a book at the end of a long day of touring. You could even stay overnight if you're looking for a quiet, out-of-the-way place to unwind. Until 1825 Långholmen was a women's prison when it became the main prison in Stockholm and

SWING BY FOR AN EVENT

With its proximity to Gamla Stan and major entertainment venues, not to mention the quiet charm of the island itself, home rentals in Södermalm are no longer the cheaper alternative to staying in a hotel. Many events happen near Södermalm or in the Trädgården, but large arenas like the Avicii Arena and the Strawberry Arena in Ulriksdal host the biggest concerts and events. Unfortunately, Södermalm is no longer cheap, so if you're coming into town for an event, you could stay in outlying districts like Ulriksdal and Solna, which are very well served by public transport. Plus you can always enjoy breakfast at a hotel without having to cook it yourself.

then was formally transformed into a publicly accessible pleasure island for football, kayaking and picnics for the people of the city in 1989. Today the island is a picturesque mishmash of perfectly preserved buildings from earlier times and modern sporting facilities. The 30-minute walk around the island is worth it for a taste of old Stockholm.

Folkoperan

MUSIC VENUE

MAP: 6 P88 C2

Opera for the people! This is the rallying cry of the **Folkoperan** (*folkoperan.se*), an antidote to the stuffy formality of other opera venues around the world and dedicated to allowing ordinary folks to enjoy this unique art. The great thing about opera is that most aficionados rarely understand the language of the performance anyway, so whether you speak Swedish or not, if this is a genre that you are curious about, the Folkoperan is a good place to experience it. Read the performance description online in advance though as some of the presentations can be a little risqué for younger audiences.

Old-Fashioned Eats

EATING

MAP: 7 P88 F4

You're in Sweden and you want to know what a Swedish meatball tastes like outside your local IKEA. Head to **Pelikan** (*pelikan.se*), a restaurant that has stood on its current site for over 100 years. But Pelikan is more than a restaurant, it's a monument to a Sweden that no longer exists and is one of the best places in Stockholm to try Swedish cuisine. The great hall has towered over tired diners for 120 years as they've been served venison fillets and local beers down below. Today's menu is rich in meal options and positively wealthy when it comes to drinks, making this a great stop for

FESTIVAL CITY

The people of Stockholm love to put on a festival, and visitors come from the region and further afield in Europe and even North America to catch events here because they are well supported by accommodation and public transport. Libraries, museums and galleries across the city stay open well into the night for free as part of Kulturnatt Stockholm (kulturnattstockholm.se). Enjoy the latest Swedish acts and some of the most popular international names at Stockholm Jazz Festival (stockholmjazz.se). Get a taste of Scandinavian design trends during Stockholm Design Week (stockholmdesignweek.se). Ötillö Swimrun (otilloswimrun.com) is a popular endurance duathlon that crosses much of the city into the archipelago.

HOME OF POP MUSIC

From the moment that the ABBA quartet hopped onto the Eurovision stage in 1974, popular music has been one of Sweden's best-known exports. Familiar names include the '90s group Ace of Base, dance icon Robyn and EDM legend Avicii. Swedish songwriters are also hugely influential and behind big hits for superstars like Rihanna and One Direction. The lyrics don't always make sense, but they do always catch on and get you dancing, which is probably more important.

just a sip. There are also more vegan options today, but this is definitely a meat-forward restaurant. Reservations are recommended for dinner.

Let's Go Clubbing! ENTERTAINMENT

MAP: 8 P88 **F2**

One thing Sweden is known for is its club culture, as the origin of some of the most celebrated club DJs and performers. While in Södermalm, you have two choices – you could head out on your own and try to find some recommendations from people that you meet, or you could drop by the **Södra Teatern** (*sodrateatern.com*) on a Friday or Saturday for one of their renowned club nights in a building that has hosted entertainment since 1859. If you do the latter, you can even say it was a cultural experience and not merely a night out. And if clubbing isn't your thing, enjoy more relaxed drinks and bites on the terrace in the summer.

Tantolunden PARK

MAP: 9 P88 **A3**

Winter days in Stockholm are long and often rainy, so it makes sense that when the sun comes out in the summer, residents flock to the city's open spaces to catch a little of the sun's magic. **Tantolunden** is the largest park in Södermalm and during the summer it feels like a large festival. The outdoor gym and children's play areas are an enormous attraction for locals and a useful place if your hotel has no gym of its own. There are also some restaurants dotted throughout the park. For experienced swimmers, this is a great place for open-water swimming but note that there are no lifeguards on duty. This park is not a beach (note: there is no sand), but it does get plenty of sun, and walking along the the paths close to the water at sunset is a spellbinding experience. And in the winter, the gentle slopes of the park are excellent for sledging.

NAVIGATING SÖDERMALM

Don't be fooled by the maps – Södermalm is the largest of Stockholm's main islands and it is a challenge to navigate the entire island only on foot. Get the SL travel card and use it, particularly if your destinations are on the east-west axis of the island.

New Slussen PARK

It's hard to ignore the construction that's happening at the edge of Södermalm so let's talk about it. Slated for completion in 2025, this major project involves turning the water's edge between Södermalm and Gamla Stan into a transportation hub and gathering place. **Slussen** is named after the lock that regulates the flow of water between the Baltic Sea and Lake Mälaren. Last updated in 1935, the lock has been rebuilt to reflect more stringent environmental standards and to cope with rising sea levels; there's also a new road bridge from Gamla Stan to Södermalm. New Slussen's bus station is being carved out from within the Katarina bedrock, and will have direct new connections with the metro and commuter rail lines. Overlooking the waterfront will be the new Katarina Park. The lock itself doubles as a plaza with pedestrian and cycle lanes connecting Stockholm's two central islands and is already open. You can bring your sandwich and drink here for a break between stops.

See p88 for map of locations

Best Places for...

€ Budget €€ Midrange €€€ Top End

Eating

Swedish Food

Pelikan €€
See 7 F4
Classic home cooking. The herring options are particularly good. *pelikan.se; 11.30am–1am*

Blå Dorren €€
10 E1
Beautifully executed Swedish classics under 17th-century ceilings. *bla-dorren.se; 10.30am-11pm Mon & Tue, 1pm-midnight Wed & Thu, 1pm–1am Fri & Sat, 1-11pm Sun*

High-End Dining

Celeste €€€
11 C2
Book for the set menu or the seasonally curated bar menu. *celesterestaurant.se; 5pm-1am Thu-Sun*

Bar Agrikultur €€€
12 G4
Award-winning cuisine focused on celebrating Swedish produce. *baragrikultur.com; 5-10pm Sun-Thu, to 11 pm Fri & Sat*

Drinking

Wines

Dryck Vinbar
13 D2
Wine bar with a broad selection. *dryckvinbar.se; 4pm –11pm, Tue-Sat*

Brännerian Bar
14 H3
Sustainable bar that tries to make all its drinks and mixers on-site. *brannerian.se; 5-11pm Wed-Thu, to midnight Fri & Sat*

Beers

Södra Teatern
See 8 F2
Multifunctional culture palace with a terrace providing dazzling city views and a club. *sodrateatern.com; hours vary*

Kvarnen
15 F3
Traditional Swedish food and drink with lots of beer. *kvarnen.com; 11am-midnight Mon & Tue, to 3am Wed-Fri, 11.30am-3am Sat, 11.30am-11pm Sun*

Shopping

Judits
16 B2
Pre-loved fashion. *judits.se; 11am-6pm Mon-Fri, to 4.30pm Sat, noon-4pm Sun*

Humana
17 C2
Secondhand fashion. *humanasecondhand.se; 11am-7pm M-F; 6pm Sat, noon-5pm Sun*

Artikel 2
18 E1
Non-profit selling preloved goods. *artikel2.se; 10am-7pm Mon-Fri, from 11am Sat, noon-6pm Sun*

Kaolin
19 D1
Pure ceramics gallery. *kaolin.se; 11am-6pm Tue-Fri, to 4pm Sat, noon-4pm Sun*

Konsthantverkarna
20 E1
Textiles and ceramics. *konsthantverkarna.se; 11am-6pm Mon-Fri, to 4pm Sat*

World of Craft
21 D1
Worldwide artisans. *aworldofcraft.se; 10.30am-6pm M-F, 11am-5pm Sat, noon-4pm Sun*

See p112
for eating, drinking and shopping listings

Explore Östermalm

Östermalm is Stockholm at its most luxurious. Bustling Stureplan, famous for its oddball rain shelter 'Svampen' (Mushroom), is surrounded by long-standing celebrity hangouts. Flanking the plaza is Birger Jarlsgatan, a veritable runway of luxe fashion boutiques. Östermalm has excellent museums and the city's most illustrious theatre, the Dramaten. The parklands of Ladugårdsgärdet, part of the Royal National City Park, host several great museums and countless Stockholmers running, walking or biking. Norra Djurgården is home to Stockholm University and the city's prime botanical garden. Further east on the island of Lindgö is Millesgården, the wonderful sculpture garden, gallery and former home of artist Carl Milles.

Getting Around

Bus

Karlaplan is the most central landmark to navigate towards in Östermalm and the number 1 bus drops you within five minutes of Östermalm Saluhall.

Metro

The 13 tunnelbana goes directly from T-Centraalen to Karlaplan. Get off at Östermalmstorg station and you'll be within three minutes of the Saluhall.

Tram

The 7 tram will get you close to the Ladugårdsgärdet museums.

THE BEST

MUSEUM
Historiska Museet (p104)

PARK
Ladugårdsgärdet (p100)

SMALL MUSEUM
Millesgården (p111)

ARCHITECTURAL WONDER
Östermalm Saluhall (p110)

SWEDISH FOOD
Lisa Elmqvist (p112)

Östermalm Saluhall (p110)

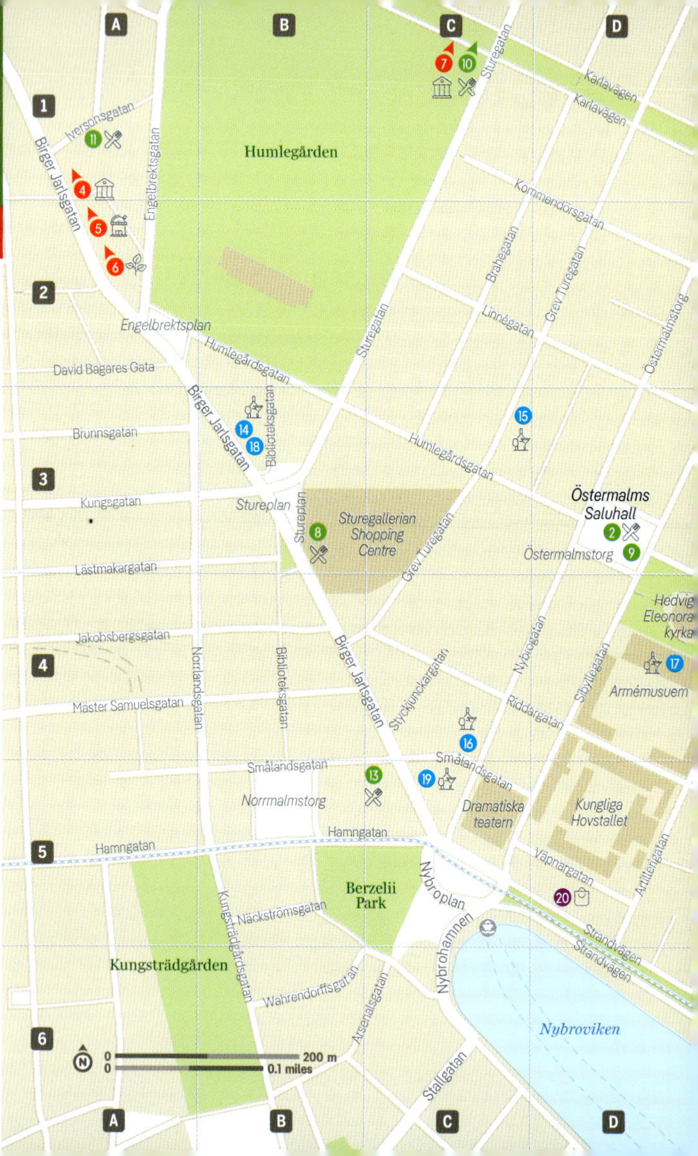
A
B
C
D
1
2
3
4
5
6
Humlegården
Iversonsgatan
Birger Jarlsgatan
Engelbrektsgatan
Sturegatan
Karlavägen
Kommendörsgatan
Brahegatan
Grev Turegatan
Linnégatan
Östermalmstorg
Engelbrektsplan
Humlegårdsgatan
David Bagares Gata
Brunnsgatan
Biblioteksgatan
Kungsgatan
Stureplan
Sturegallerian Shopping Centre
Östermalms Saluhall
Lästmakargatan
Hedvig Eleonora kyrka
Jakobsbergsgatan
Nybrogatan
Sibyllegatan
Armémusuem
Norrlandsgatan
Mäster Samuelsgatan
Styckjunkargatan
Riddargatan
Smålandsgatan
Norrmalmstorg
Dramatiska teatern
Kungliga Hovstallet
Hamngatan
Väpnargatan
Artillerigatan
Berzelii Park
Nybroplan
Näckströmsgatan
Kungsträdgårdsgatan
Nybrohamnen
Strandvägen
Kungsträdgården
Wahrendorffsgatan
Arsenalsgatan
Nybroviken
Stallgatan
0 200 m
0 0.1 miles

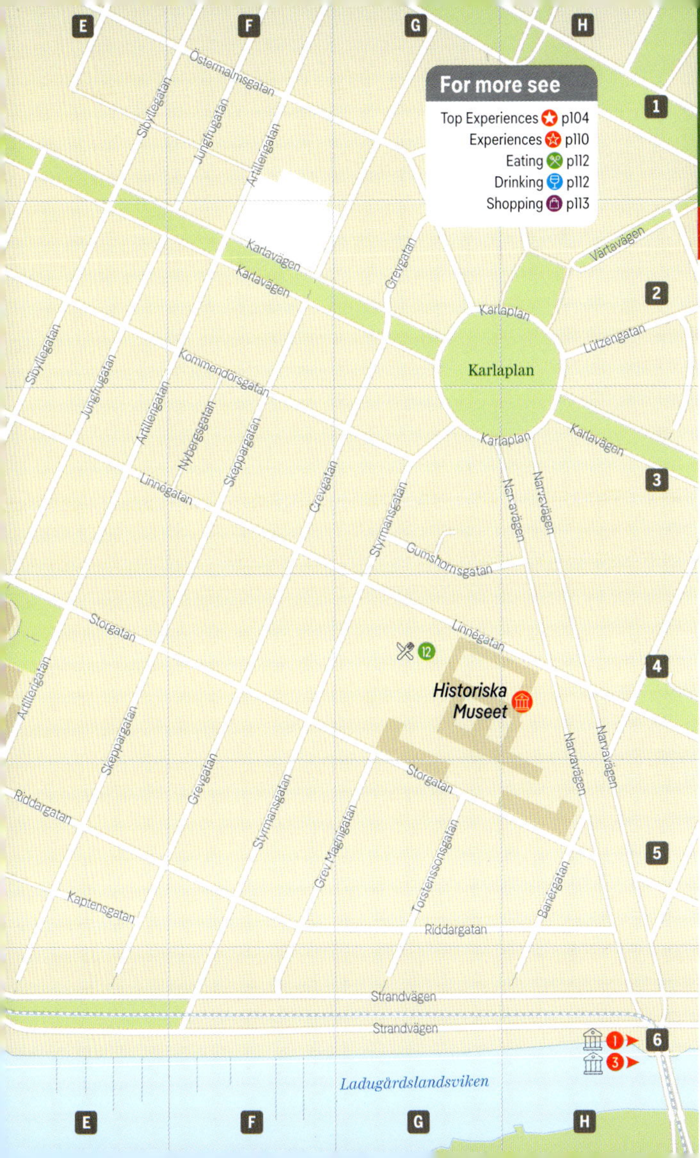

For more see
Top Experiences p104
Experiences p110
Eating p112
Drinking p112
Shopping p113

★ TOP EXPERIENCE

Historiska Museet

What is Sweden anyway? This is the question that is at the centre of the **Historiska Museet** that brings together artefacts spanning more than 10,000 years of history. It is a story of conquest, resistance, creativity and a constant search for unity, including finally emphasising Sami histories for visitors.

MAP P103 **H4**

PLANNING TIP
The annual pass (450kr) available on-site is cheaper than two separate tickets for any of the seven museums under the National Historical Museums umbrella.

Scan this QR code to learn more about the annual pass and the National Historical Museums.

Gold Room

Guilder. Dahab. Bling. Just about every culture in the world that has come into contact with gold has a nickname for the precious metal, and the Swedes are no exception.

One of the most visited rooms in the museum, and an undisputed highlight, the subterranean Gold Room brings together artefacts from Swedish history made from the world's most coveted metal, from the moment people from continental Europe migrated into the Nordic region to the present, including a few objects from the indigenous Sami community.

The lighting and dark decor make the entire gleaming space even more evocative – you really get a sense of why this shiny metal fascinates the human mind.

Unvarnished Histories

For a country that today has a reputation as a haven of peace and tranquility, Sweden has a pretty gory and bloody past. The Historiska Museet doesn't shy away from telling this part of history,

JONATHAN SMITH/SHUTTERSTOCK ©

whether through Viking raids or regal bloodbaths as noble families vied for dominance.

The Medieval Massacre room commemorates one such chapter around the 1361 Battle of Gotland, which was one of the formative battles against Danish conquest that knitted together the country as we know it today. Unfortunately, the locals lost that one, though these farmers and even the children of the island didn't go down without a spirited fight. Archaeological studies have led to a clearer picture of what happened – some 1800 were thrown into mass graves outside Visby – and the display, though gruesome, is fascinating.

If you or someone in your party is fascinated by shows like *Game of Thrones*, you'll appreciate this installation but, remember, this was all real.

QUICK BREAK
The museum restaurant serves great meals and has a dedicated children's menu.

Medieval History

In our current time its very hard to believe that Christianity was once so deeply intertwined with people's lives in Europe that it was criminal to do things like work on holy days. Sweden was one of the most religious countries in Europe. But it's true, and in the 'medieval' rooms you can learn more about what it meant to live under such strict rules. There are two rooms dedicated to medieval life – one to art and the other to everyday objects; both are worth a gander. Plus, with the closure of the Medieval Museum pending the identification of a new location, much of that museum's collection has been loaned to the Historiska Museet to enhance its already extensive holdings.

BERK OZDEMIR/SHUTTERSTOCK ©

Economy Museum

'Economy' is such a buzzword in politics and in the news, but do any of us really understand what it is? Entry to the Historiska Museet also includes admission to the Economy Museum, which is in the same complex, so you can learn more about what an economy actually is.

As well as coins, banknotes and other objects that have been used for trade, there are also deeply fascinating installations that really help to explain how the different strands of this thing called the economy come together. It shouldn't take more than an hour to visit the whole place, and more in-depth activities are regularly scheduled for kids too.

GHOSTS OF VIKINGS PAST

Vikings are the rock stars of European history. You can tell because people come to Sweden, and this museum specifically, just to learn more about who the Vikings were and how they lived.

WALKING TOUR

Ladugårdsgärdet

Östermalm is a bit of a sleepy district that's great for shopping and walking around, but every weekend Ladugårdsgärdet (the garden district) comes alive with people from all over the city trying to get their ten thousand steps in any which way they can. Join them!

START	END	LENGTH
Karlaplan	Hundudden	5km; 1½ to two hours

1 Ring Around the Roses

Karlaplan, one of Stockholm's main roundabouts, also doubles as a small park with an extensive walking path flowing from it. In summer, the benches surrounded by bee-filled blossoms are an excellent place to sit with a sandwich and people-watch.

2 Historical Crossing

Take Narvavägen down towards the water and the **Djurgårdsbron** bridge that connects Östermalm to Djurgården. The restaurant under the bridge serves great food and drinks all year round and the bridge has an excellent view of the Blå Porten gate.

3 A Walk in the Park

Named for a house that was never built, **Nobelparken** is great if not particularly spectacular and has a few animal sculptures installed to entertain children. It's a good place for a break with a view of the water.

4 Tribute to the Sea

Enjoy a leisurely walk along the water for several minutes until you come to the Museiparken sign and the large building on your left is the **Sjöhistorika Museet** (Maritime History Museum). This imposing building contains collections dedicated to Sweden's military and sea-faring history, including a decent collection of boats from various eras.

5 Technically Great

Within the same area as the Sjöhistorika Museet is the **Tekniska Museet** (p110), another excellent museum worth a visit. Celebrating technology in the broadest sense of the word, this museum and its interactive installations will reward any curious visitor handsomely.

6 Out with the Old

With the water behind you, walk towards the main road onto **Djurgårdsbrunnsvägen** and follow the curve of the road until it leads back to the water's edge and the disused Djurgårdsbrunnsbron bridge, a 19th-century swing bridge that was built for the same exhibition that led to the building of the Nordiska Museet.

7 In with the New

Walk along the water until you get to the small picturesque pedestrian bridge known as **Lilla Sjötullsbron** that connects Ladugårdsgärdet to Djurgården, with its charming Instagram-worthy views over the two islands, particularly when the flowers are in bloom.

8 Looking Out over the Water

Follow the paths along the water until you get to the **Hundudden** viewpoint, which offers stunning views across the water, particularly at sunset.

EXPERIENCES

The Art of Technology

MUSEUM

MAP: 1 P102 **H6**

If a great museum is one that leaves you with many questions and answers, then **Tekniska Museet** *(tekniskamuseet.se; weekdays/weekends 100/170kr under-7s free)* is a great museum. Dedicated to technology, it provokes, inspires and illuminates visitors of all ages. There really is something for curious people of all ages here, whether you want to wander around and learn, or sit still and listen. Gamers should definitely check out the Play on Play installation – an entire floor dedicated to video games from the past, present and future as you get to try games that are still under development. It's hard to say how much time you should dedicate here, but a half-day spent here would not be wasted.

Food, Glorious Food

FOOD

MAP: 2 P102 **D3**

The title 'food hall' feels like a bit of a misnomer here. **Östermalms Saluhall** is technically a food hall, but if you're after fish and chips wrapped in newspaper you'd be better served elsewhere. This food hall features three-course prix-fixe menus and various caviars. The food is delicious and explains why this has been a mainstay in Östermalm for 130 years. **Lisa Elmqvist** (p112) is popular with diners from nearby offices for after-work drinks. The restaurants remain open until late, but if you're shopping for deli items you'll need to get here before 7pm on weekdays and 5pm on weekends. It also has unique architecture that has been restored to be period-correct – guided tours are available from a vendor by emailing lina@bielstencompany.se.

Changes Are Underway

MUSEUM

MAP: 3 P102 **H6**

Nestled within the Ladugårdsgärdet museum quarter is the **Etnografiska Museet** *(etnografiskamuseet.se; adult/child 150kr/free)*. It is fair to say that ethnography is a contested discipline, with many challenging the idea of Europeans travelling the world, categorising cultures and studying them. So a museum dedicated to that discipline may not be to everyone's taste. But this is a museum that has definitely heard that challenge and presents information more as learning about others rather than accusing them of being strange.

NORRA DJURGÅRDEN

Östermalm is the largest of Sweden's districts and is difficult to navigate end-to-end on foot. Norra Djurgården refers to the northern parts on the eastern banks of Brunnsviken lake and includes the University of Stockholm and the botanical garden. The easiest way to navigate by public transport is to head for Universitet station by tunnelbana or bus, or you can cycle along the paths that connect the two areas. The walk around Brunnsviken is particularly pleasant on summer days.

ONE TICKET, FOUR MUSEUMS

The Etnografiska Museet is part of a network of four museums – the Etnografiska Museet, Medelhavsmuseet and Östasiatiska Museet in Stockholm, and the Världskultur Museet in Gothenburg – known as the Museums of World Culture. A single ticket to enter any of these museums costs 150kr, but an annual pass for 250kr gets you entry into all four and is valid for a year.

Nature Comes Alive

MUSEUM

Biology nerds will love the **Naturhistoriska Riksmuseet** (MAP: 4 P102 A1, *nrm.se; adult/child 160kr/free*), founded by Carl von Linné, better known by his Latinised name Karolus Linneus or the 'father of modern taxonomy'. The short version is that this is the guy who decided we should name animals, plants and other living things using two Latin names that tell us more about the genetic family the specimen belongs to. Under the charge of the University of Stockholm, the **Museum of Natural History** (MAP: 5 P102 A2) has continued a tradition of learning and teaching that includes some of the coolest interactive exhibitions in the city. Cosmonova is an especially big draw for the young and the young at heart; it's an IMAX projection on an enormous screen that immerses viewers in the world of asteroids or the deep-blue sea. Separate tickets are required – bring your own headphones for English narration.

A Walk in the Garden

BOTANICAL GARDEN

Take a break from the hustle and bustle of travel in the far north of Norra Djurgården at the oldest botanical garden in Sweden known as **Bergianska Trädgården** (MAP: 6 P102 A2, Bergius Botanic Garden). As far as botanical gardens go, it's pretty standard fare with spaces dedicated to Sweden's niche sub-systems, as well as Italian, and Japanese-style terraces and ponds, and collections from other parts of the world. But it still remains a pleasant year-round destination for anyone looking to spend time outdoors.

A Monument to Love

MUSEUM

MAP: 7 P102 C1

Over the bridge on the island of Lidingö is the **Millesgården** (*millesgarden.se; adult/child 170kr/free*), a curious but fascinating small museum that is both a tribute to the strength of a marriage and the power of art to turn the most banal spaces into a destination. Carl and Olga Milles put many of the details of this small museum together themselves. Spend time in the sculpture garden especially that draws from architectural cultures across Europe and offers excellent views of the city from the clifftop. There's also a great cafe on-site.

LISTINGS

Best Places for...

€ Budget €€ Midrange €€€ Top End

See p102 for map of locations

Eating

Seafood

Sturehof €€
8 B3
Superb for late-night dining, this convivial brasserie serves fabulous seafood-centric dishes and has views onto Stureplan. *sturehof.com; 11.30am-2am Mon-Sat, from noon Sun*

Lisa Elmqvist €€
9 D3
So popular with the locals that you know it's good, within the Östermalms Saluhall. *lisaelmqvist.se; 9.30am-7pm Mon-Fri, to 5pm Sat*

Fika

Millesgården Lanthandel €€
10 C1
Within the grounds of the Millesgården; serves excellent tea and pastries. *millesgarden lanthandel.se; 11am-5pm Tue-Sun*

Café Saturnus €€
11 C1
French-inspired menu with great pastries and also full meals. *cafesaturnus.se; 8am-7pm Mon-Fri, from 9am Sat & Sun*

Sustainable Dining

Restaurang Oxenstiernan €€
12 G4
Sustainable gastronomy at this dining gem next to an Östermalm park. In summer, dine alfresco under trees. *oxenstiernan.se; 5-10pm Tue-Sat*

Konstnärsbaren €€€
13 C5
An Östermalm classic since 1931, oozing an arty bohemian atmosphere especially in its mural-covered bar. *konstnarsbaren.se; 11.30am-11pm Mon & Tue, to midnight Wed-Fri, noon-midnight Sat*

Drinking

Upmarket Drinks

Lucy's Flower Shop
14 B3
Not a florist, but a moodily lit, velvet-upholstered basement bar serving creative cocktails. Bookings are advised. *lucysstockholm.se; 5pm-1am Tue-Sun*

Bar Called Gemma
15 C3
Trendy and working hard at being laid-back with great drinks and themed nights; ranked as one of the 50 best bars in the world. *abarcalledgemma.se; 3pm-12.30am Mon-Sat*

Teatergrillen
16 C4
Another popular spot for Swedish celebrities with decor inspired by a nearby theatre. Wear your nice jeans. *teatergrillen.se; 11.30am-11pm Mon & Tue, to midnight Wed & Thu, to 1am Fri & Sat*

MIKAEL DAMKIER/SHUTTERSTOCK ©

Stjärtilleriet

17 **D4**

Experimental cocktails and refreshing irregularity in a part of the city that sometimes takes itself too seriously. *stjartilleriet.se; 5pm-midnight Tue-Thu, 4pm-1am Fri & Sat*

Clubbing

Spy Bar

18 **B3**

Stockholm's most famous nightclub attracts the who's who of the city. Queues are long. *stureplansgruppen.se/nightlife/spy-bar; 11pm-5am Thu-Sat*

Lilla Baren at Riche

19 **C5**

A darling of Östermalm's hip parade, Lilla Baren mixes smooth bar staff, skilled DJs and a fashion-literate crowd. *riche.se/lilla-baren; 11.30am-3pm Mon, to midnight Tue, to 2am Wed-Sat*

Shopping

Odds & Ends

Östermalms Saluhall

See 2 D3

High-end deli items from across Sweden including caviars and seasonal fish (pictured). *ostermalmshallen.se; 9.30am-7pm Mon-Fri, to 5pm Sat*

Svenskt Tenn

20 **D5**

Swedish-made homewares and furnishings, including an impressive range of ornaments and knick-knacks. *svenskttenn.com; 10am-6pm Mon-Fri, to 5pm Sat, 11am-4pm Sun*

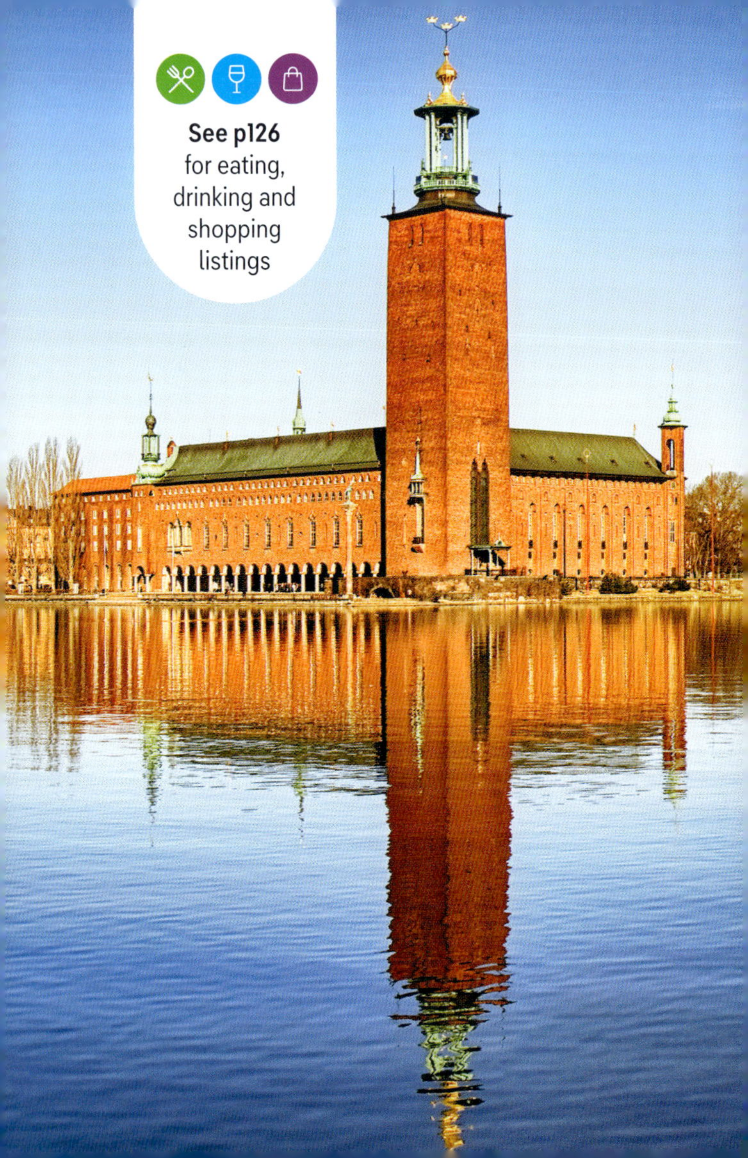

See p126 for eating, drinking and shopping listings

Explore Kungsholmen

Kungsholmen has come a long way since it was nicknamed 'Starvation Island' during the 19th century, when putrid factories, poverty and disease were everywhere. Today it's all about revamped industrial buildings and gentrification. Architectural blockbuster Stadshuset (City Hall) dominates the east end of the island. From there, the island unfolds in a mix of offices and housing until the purely residential districts on the western reaches. The beach at Smedsuddsbadet fills up with sunbathers in the summer and is a great place for an open-water swim, while Rålambshovsparken is ideal for a picnic, for sunbathers and for dog-walkers alike.

Getting Around

Metro

The Centralstationen and T-Centralen tunnelbana station get you close to Stadhuset. The island itself is a little bigger than it looks on the map so you can also take the tunnelbana to Rådhuset for a short walk from the island and to see the remarkable station or to Kristineberg for attractions on the western side of the island.

Walk

Kungsholmen's main attractions are within walking distance from Gamla Stan. Most of the parks are connected via a walking and cycling path along the water.

Stadshuset (p117)

THE BEST

ARCHITECTURAL WONDER
Stadshuset (p117)

URBAN BEACH
Smedsuddsbadet (p122)

PARK
Rålambshovsparken (p122)

SMALL CAFE
Café Portiken (p126)

SUSTAINABLE DINING
Lux Dag för Dag (p124)

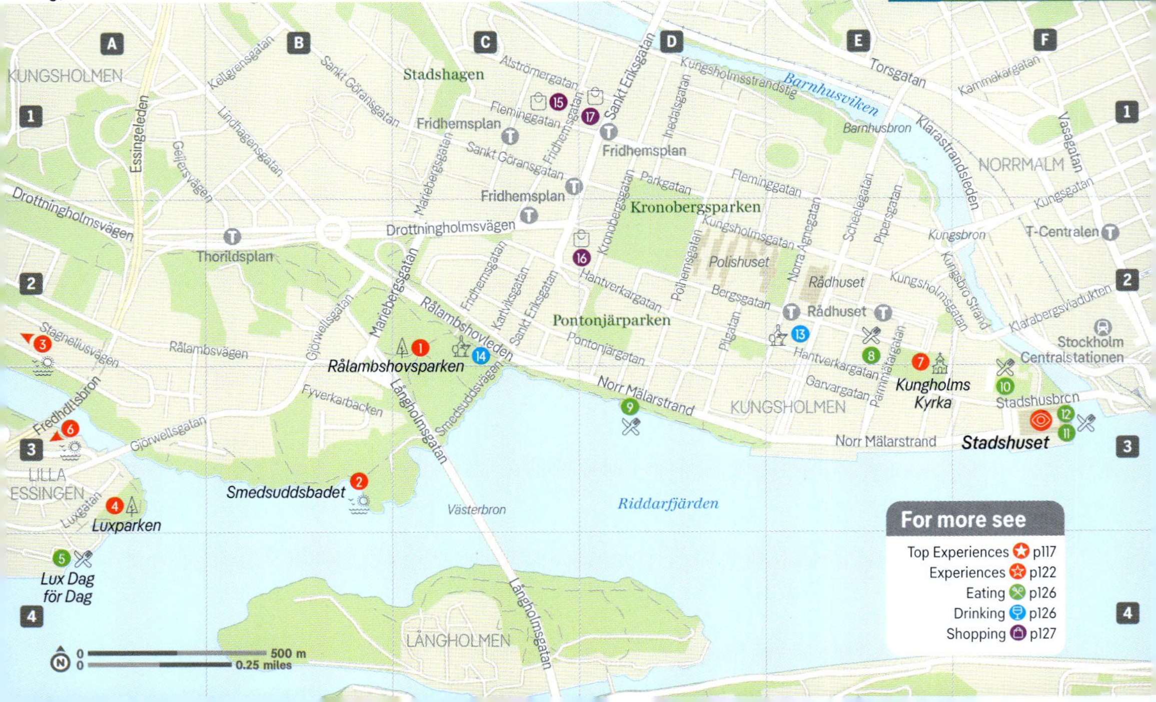
Stadshagen
Fridhemsplan
Kronobergsparken
Polishuset
Rådhuset
Pontonjärparken
Rålambshovsparken
Smedsuddsbadet
Luxparken
Lux Dag för Dag
Kungholms Kyrka
Stadshuset
Stockholm Centralstationen
Riddarfjärden
Barnhusviken
KUNGSHOLMEN
NORRMALM
LILLA ESSINGEN
LÅNGHOLMEN
Thoridsplan
Västerbron
For more see
Top Experiences p117
Experiences p122
Eating p126
Drinking p126
Shopping p127
500 m
0.25 miles

★ TOP EXPERIENCE

Stadshuset

The seat of government in Stockholm could not be a more impressive building. Unlike other cities where municipal buildings are staid, brutalist affairs or grandiose neoclassical monuments, the **Stadshuset** in Stockholm is a stunning, redbrick edifice built in a uniquely Swedish style. It's impressive, even before you encounter the marvels inside.

Singular Architecture

If you're walking from Gamla Stan, your first sight of Kungsholmen is the redbrick city hall that is Stadshuset, designed by Ragnar Östberg and completed in 1923. Entry to the building is by guided tour, lasting around 50 minutes with tours starting in the entryway furthest from the street. English tours usually take place on the hour between 10am and 3pm daily. There's no need to book in advance, but you do need to check the website as there are fewer tours during the winter months.

This building is considered the pinnacle of Swedish National Romantic style and draws hundreds of visitors even though it is very much an active office building. Around 350 city bureaucrats work here and numerous events like the annual Nobel Prize banquet are held in its enormous Blue Hall each December. Drop by on the weekend and you'll find it's also a very popular place to get married.

The building's stern facade hides many remarkable secrets, including the courtyard that immediately unfolds from the main entrance. Surrounded by high arches and redbrick walls, this space still

MAP P116 **F3**

PLANNING TIP
There are only 27 tickets issued each day during the summer for the clocktower, so if you're after views from above, arrive early.

Scan this QR code to book tickets for the tower (summer only).

QUICK BREAK
There are a couple of good options for dining at Stadshuset. Join the city employees at the **Ragnars Skafferi** cafe (p126) for a great-value buffet lunch. Or dine like a Nobel Prize winner in Stadshuset's handsomely decorated basement restaurant, **Stadshuskällaren** (p126), where you can go à la carte or order the same menu as was served at the previous year's Nobel Prize banquet.

manages to feel open and inviting because of the garden and open water nearby.

Seat of Government

At the centre the Stadshuset is Blå Hallen (Blue Hall). It's a cavernous chamber that rises many floors, but even the least observant person will quickly notice that it is not blue. The architect designed it to look like a vast Italian loggia with high arches and large windows; a secret interior courtyard rising four storeys high still feels open because of the row of open windows close to the ceilings and the birds that occasionally flutter through it. The dramatic staircase rises up to the arches above and makes an imposing backdrop for the ceremonies that are held here; its pale colours contrasting with the red against the walls.

Golden Marvel

The highlight of the guided tour is the Golden Hall, a dazzling floor-to-ceiling design by Einar Forseth incorporating some 18 million gilded mosaic pieces. You may audibly gasp when you see it for the first time, particularly if it's lit up. It's difficult to capture the grand opulence of this room with its towering ceilings and gilt murals that tell stories of key moments in Swedish history.

People at Work

The guided tour will also take you to the other side of the courtyard where the council chambers are just as impressive as the ceremonial rooms. The Rådsalen (Red Room) is the council chamber where decisions about the management of the city are made, with a soaring vaulted and painted ceiling that conveys the weight of the decisions made here. The guided tour also takes you to the Prins Eugen Gallery with its beautiful panoramic mural of the city skyline, painted by Gustav V's talented brother.

ADISA/SHUTTERSTOCK ©

Garden Walk

City Hall's lakeside park is pretty in all seasons, and offers stunning views of Riddarholmen and Södermalm across the water. In keeping with the open traditions of Swedish government, it's not uncommon to find sunbathers and readers here whenever the sun peeks out from behind the clouds. Pay attention to the sculptures – there are two statues by Carl Eldh that guard the steps, and Christian Eriksson's *Engelbrekt the Freedom Fighter* graces a pillar in the corner of the park.

Towering Heights

You'll need a separate ticket to climb the 106m tower (Jun-end Aug) of which there are only 27 issued for each session. It offers stellar views and a great thigh workout on its 365 steps.

WALKING TOUR

Kungsholmen

Kungsholmen is primarily a residential district and most of the interesting buildings are office buildings that are not necessarily geared towards tourists. This walk is designed to give you a feel for the neighbourhood rather than a list of sites.

START	END	LENGTH
Stadshuset	Rådhuset tunnelbana	2km; one hour

1 Stadsuhuset

Start at the **Stadshuset** (p117) and take the free guided tour if it's available to you. Don't forget to walk down by the water for excellent views of both the architecture of the building and the islands across the water.

2 Café Portiken

On Hantverkargatan walk a few metres to **Café Portiken** (p126), where you can get affordable meals including soups and sandwiches for as little as 100kr. This is a great place to unwind after a tour of the Stadshuset and to regroup before taking on the rest of the island.

3 Kungholms Kyrkan

Stay on Hantverkargatan for the 17th-century **Kungholms Kyrkan** (p124), which is one of the largest churches on the island. The austere decor is a sharp contrast to the opulence of many churches from Sweden's Catholic period but the paintings of saints and famous donors on the walls are interesting examples of the period's style.

4 Stockholm County Council

Continuing on Hantverkagatan you'll come by a large building that's set a little further back from the edge of the street in simple but perfectly manicured gardens. This is the **Stockholm County Council** building – the county administers the outlying residential districts of Stockholm.

5 Stockholm District Court

Looping back onto Hantverkagatan and then Scheelegatan. you'll arrive at the **Stockholm District Court**. It's a very simple building but actually represents the same National Romantic style of architecture as the Stadshuset that emerged in Sweden in the late 19th century, even though this building is a less interesting example.

6 Polishusparken

The small grounds of the Rådhuset to the west are known as the **Polishusparken**. Pictures are discouraged here because the imposing neoclassical building nearby is the headquarters of the police and there's a prison inside, but this is a beautiful garden where you can rest your feet after a day of touring.

7 Rådhuset Tunnelbana

Finish your walk at one of the most interesting tunnelbana stations in Stockholm. The **Rådhuset station** is designed to feel like it was carved right into the rock.

EXPERIENCES

Promenade by the Water

WALK

The walk between **Stadshuset** and the **Rålambshovparken** is one of the most pleasant walks in Stockholm, with beautiful sunsets and views over the water. Start in the gardens of the Stadshuset and walk out through the small gate towards Kungsholmen and then just stay on the path. You'll pass by some public docks used by small boating companies that ferry commuters from the small outer islands and from numerous bars and restaurants where you can grab sundowners. Boats to the outer island of Mariefred also leave from here. The path eventually circumnavigates the island so if you're running or biking, this is a great activity for one to two hours, but keep in mind that you'll need to come inland at certain points. Watch out for other runners at sunset – it gets a little crowded in the summer.

Park Yourself Here

PARK

MAP: 1 P116 C2

Stockholm is, in general, a dog-friendly city, although dogs are not allowed in most museums unless they are service animals. One place where furry friends gather in their masses is at **Rålambshovsparken**, a large open park that you access easily by walking along the boardwalk. The sunsets here are also very impressive and on a particularly hot day it can fill up quite quickly and food trucks come down to join the fun. It's a great place to relax and end the day even if you don't have a dog with you. There are a few interesting sculptures, some boules fields and a skatepark as well. Fun fact: this was also the park where Greta Thunberg's 'Fridays for Future' climate protests were started.

WATER QUALITY

Stockholm sits in a large estuary and, generally speaking, the water west of Gamla Stan is said to be ocean water and east is Mälaren, a large freshwater lake. In theory swimming in Lake Mälaren is possible across the various bathing sites are managed by the municipality in the summer, but water quality varies across sites due to the high presence of things like bird droppings as many pigeons and geese gather to eat rubbish that people fail to dispose of properly. The water quality is measured daily in the summer and notices are placed on the site if it's poor or if swimming has been suspended.

URBAN GETAWAY

In the summer, the ferry to the historical Mariefred island leaves from the docks near Stadshuset. You can purchase tickets on the ferries and there's a dining car on board.

Beach Day

URBAN BEACH

MAP: 2 P116 B3

Smedsuddsbadet is one of the most popular beaches in Stockholm, but this is not a 'beach' in the popular sense of the word – if you're looking for white sand and waves, you will not find them here. And unlike other urban beaches, the city of Stockholm does not go out of its way to create such illusions – there's no massive deposit of sand that might alter the local ecosystem so that visitors can pretend to be somewhere else. What it is is a great place to catch some rays and meet up with other people while enjoying the sun and the outdoors. There is a sandy play area for children, deckchairs for sunbathers in the summer, and a jetty from which you can dive in the water for a swim, including a ramp to increase accessibility. Plus there are public changing facilities, which if you visit enough places in Sweden, you'll realise is not always guaranteed. Swimming is possible but may be abruptly suspended if the water quality deteriorates.

Urban Hike

NATURE TRAIL

A small nature trail connects Smedsuddsbadet to **Fredhällsklipporna**, a small rocky beach where open-water swimming is possible. Popular with nearby residents at all times of the day, there are no large animals but instead plenty for birdwatchers who can listen through the urban soundscape. Look out for the small rose garden, especially when it's in bloom in the summer. The trail is unfortunately not easily navigable for wheelchair users as there are several ascents, descents and narrow sharp turns. But if you're a trail runner or just out looking for your daily step count, this is a great and only moderately challenging extension to the shorter loop that leaves Stadshuset.

One for the Water Lovers

SWIMMING

MAP: 3 P116 A2

At the far end of the southern stretch of Kungsholmen is the **Fredhällsbadet**, an open-water swimming site that is available to members of the club year-round, and to the public during summer. A large deck makes for excellent sunbathing and sometimes groups host yoga with views of the sunset and the bridge to Alvik and Bromma. If you're training for a triathlon or are just a fan of open-water swimming, this is one of the best places in Stockholm to get your fix.

Take Your Pick

SWIMMING

MAP: 4 P116 **A3**

If you love outdoor swimming you must check out the small island of **Lilla Essingen**. It is tiny – you could easily walk around the whole island in about 20 minutes and there are only a few restaurants and shops. But the public jetties everywhere invite you to take a plunge in Lake Mälaren's cool, crisp waters. Less crowded than Smedsuddsbladet and other popular beaches because they don't get as much direct sunlight, these are nonetheless very rewarding spots if you're after a refreshing swim on a hot day. Note that there are no lifeguards on duty so children should not be allowed to swim unsupervised. Start at Luxparken on the east side of the island, which has been renovated to be more inviting to park-goers.

Far from the Madding Crowd

DINING

MAP: 5 P116 **A4**

The restaurant business can be a tough nut to crack, especially if you're not in one of the more popular areas of town. On the small residential island of Lilla Essingen, some restauranteurs decided that they would make fine dining more accessible to their neighbourhood by bringing their techniques and styles into a restaurant with a more homely feel. **Lux Dag för Dag** (p126) is a farm-to-table restaurant that celebrates Scandinavian produce and shared meals in a cosy setting. The food is good, and wine pairings are available, but it's the kind of place that is designed with food rather than vibes at the centre. Bookings are advised.

KEEPING UP WITH THE ESSINGENS

The two small islands of Lilla Essingen and Stora Essingen (literally 'Small' and 'Big' Essignen) are residential districts of Stockholm connected to the main island through pedestrian and vehicular bridges. There's not much for tourists to do in these outlying districts, but they are popular with Stockholmers who enjoy boating and open-water swimming, both of which are available year-round from jetties off the islands. For runners, visiting these islands is a great place to tag on some extra miles to your run. There is no pedestrian access to the large bridge. Instead, use the Mariebergsbron bridge from the Mareibergs park to access the pedestrian bridge and roads that connect both islands.

STOCKHOLM ON A BUDGET

Stockholm can be a relatively expensive place to visit but there are some ways that you can bring the cost down. If you're a student – regardless of age – always travel with a student card as almost all museums and cultural venues will have concessions. Some will even have special events put on for students. Take advantage of the extensive parks and green spaces with a picnic or an open-water swim. Churches and other religious institutions often put on free or subsidised concerts in venues that have tremendous acoustics and magnificent organs, and this can be a good way to pass some time. Look out for noticeboards nearby for details of coming performances.

Serious Big Sister

SWIMMING

MAP: 6 P116 **A3**

On the residential island of Stora Essingen is another beach that is worth checking out if you enjoy open-water swimming. **Oxhålsbadet** doesn't have much by way of amenities but it does have a shallow area making it one of the more child-friendly open-water swimming areas this side of Stockholm. There's also a small nature trail that you can enjoy. Stora Essingen is harder to circumnavigate than its little sister, but if you're determined, you can also navigate the inner streets to the other side of the island at Broparken where a scenic path takes you about half way around the island.

Holy Jams

CHURCH

MAP: 7 P116 **E2**

Away from the tourist circuit, the **Kungholms Kyrka** is an interesting place to take a break, especially after a tour of the Stadshuset. There are beautiful grounds where you can eat a sandwich or walk through the cemetery if that's your thing, and the austere interiors are a fascinating break from the excesses of the Stadshuset or Catholic churches of previous eras. For travellers on a budget looking for a little musical reprieve, every Thursday at 10am the church offers an organ concert with *fika* for 70kr.

Under the City

ART

The **Rådhuset tunnelbana** (P116 E2) station is one of the most iconic within a network that is already famous for being a celebration of art and the largest art gallery in the world. Opened in 1975, the station was designed to feel as if it was carved right out of the rock that geologists say is underneath the city hall. The fiery red rock echoes the redbrick of the Stadshuset building, and there are small pieces of Kungsholmen history embedded throughout so you feel as if you're boarding the tunnelbana in an archeological dig. You do need to get through the ticket turnstiles to access the good stuff, so have your SL travel card ready.

LISTINGS

See p116 for map of locations

Best Places for...

€ Budget €€ Midrange €€€ Top End

Eating

Seafood

Glupsk Bohuslan €
8 E2
Fish, but make it street food. Inspired by New England but drawing from Sweden's own fishing traditions. *glupsk.se; 11am-8pm Tue-Fri, from noon Sat, noon-4pm Sun*

Mälarpaviljongen €€
9 D3
Only open in the summer, but a great meeting point for drinks and sunsets. *ny.malarpaviljongen.se; 11.30am-11pm Tue-Fri, 5pm-midnight Sat & Sun Jun-Sep*

Affordable Eats

Lux Dag för Dag €€
See 5 A4
Farm-to-table freshness on the small island of Lilla Essingen. The number 1 bus will get you close. *luxdagfordag.se; 11.30am-2pm Tue-Fri, 5-10pm Wed-Sat*

Café Portiken €
10 F3
Quick lunchtime meals and *fika* right by the Stadshuset. Great soups and sandwiches. *9.30am-3.30pm Mon-Fri*

Ragnars Skafferi €
11 F3
Within the grounds of Stadshuset and mainly serving city workers, but a good option for budget travellers. *ragnarsskafferi.se; 11am-2pm Mon-Fri*

High-End Eats

Stadshuskällaren €€€
12 F3
Dine like a Nobel Prize winner in this restaurant that serves meals on the same crockery that is used during the ceremony. *stadshuskallarensthlm.se; 11.30am-2pm Mon-Fri, 5-11pm Wed-Sat*

Drinking

Sundowners by the Water

Mälarpaviljongen
See 9 D3
Only open in the summer and LGBTIQ-friendly. *ny.malarpaviljongen.se; 11.30am-11pm Tue-Fri, 5pm-midnight Sat & Sun Jun-Sep*

Lemon Bar
13 E2
Pub vibe that transforms into clubbing and cocktails on weekends with food available (pictured). *lemonbar.se; 5pm-3am Tue-Fri, 7pm-3am Sat*

Boulebar
14 C2
Part of a chain and only open in the summer. The drinks are great and you can enjoy some petanque with them. *boulebar.se; 10am-5pm Mon-Fri Jun-Sep*

JENLO8/SHUTTERSTOCK ©

Shopping

Second-Hand Shopping

Grandpa

15 C1

Well-curated selection of clothing and design items. *grandpastore.com; 11am–6pm Mon-Fri, to 5pm Sat, noon-4pm Sun*

Stockholm Stadsmission

16 D2

Part of a chain with sales supporting programmes to serve unhoused populations. *stadsmission.se; 10am-6.30pm Mon-Fri, to 5pm Sat, noon-4pm Sun*

Myrorna Second Hand

17 D1

Homewares and clothing, including a formidable selection of records. *myrorna.se; 10am-7pm Mon-Fri, to 5pm Sat, noon-4pm Sun*

See p140
for eating, drinking and shopping listings

Explore Vasastan

Vasastan's development didn't fully get going until towards the end of the 19th century. The modern buildings appealed to Stockholm's upwardly mobile and monied classes and this remains one of the city's most densely populated districts, with a chilled, neighbourly vibe. There are lots of excellent restaurants and shops, as well as a few interesting art galleries and cultural sights. Among these is the Stadsbiblioteket, an exceptional example of Swedish Grace architecture, and the historic studio of sculptor Carl Eldhs. About 3km north of Vasastan in Solna, is Hagaparken, designed in the English style and one of Sweden's best-preserved historical parks. Crown Princess Victoria lives here in the Haga Slott and it's all part of the expansive Royal National City Park.

Getting Around

Metro

Vasastan is a residential area that is well-served by tunnelbana stations and numerous bus connections.

Walk

Stockholm Odenplan is the most central tunnelbana stop and all the attractions are within a 20-minute walk from there, while St Eriksplan station gets you closer to Vasaparken and the western area. Note that Stockholm Odenplan commuter rail station and Odenplan tunnelbana station are a short walk apart; several buses go from the tunnelbana station.

THE BEST

PARK Hagaparken (p130)

GALLERY Sven-Harrys Konstmuseum (p137)

SMALL MUSEUM Carl Eldhs Ateljémuseum (p136)

FIKA Lillebrors bageri (p140)

ARCHITECTURAL WONDER Gustav Vasa Kyrka (p139)

Koppartälten, Hagaparken (p130)
ANNA YU/ALAMY ©

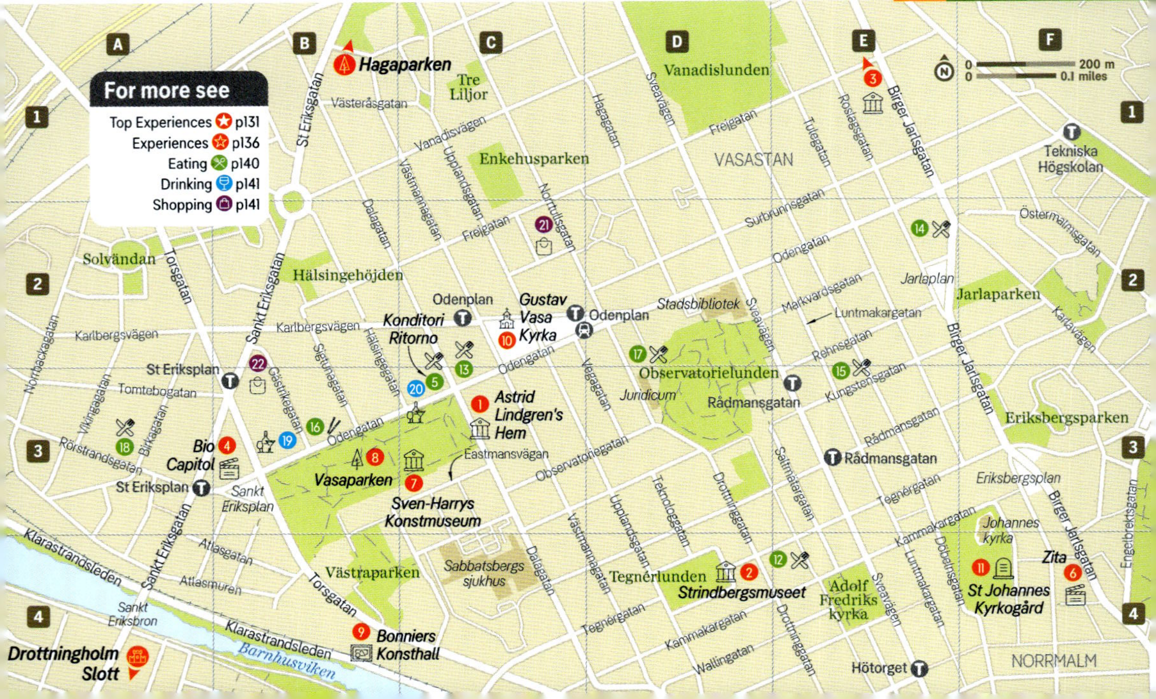
For more see
Top Experiences p131
Experiences p136
Eating p140
Drinking p141
Shopping p141
Hagaparken
Tre Liljor
Vanadislunden
VASASTAN
Enkehusparken
Hälsingehöjden
Solvändan
Tekniska Högskolan
Jarlaparken
Jarlaplan
Stadsbibliotek
Odenplan
Gustav Vasa Kyrka
Konditori Ritorno
Observatorielunden
Juridicum
Rådmansgatan
Eriksbergsparken
Eriksbergsplan
Astrid Lindgren's Hem
Vasaparken
Sven-Harrys Konstmuseum
Bio Capitol
St Eriksplan
Sankt Eriksplan
Västraparken
Sabbatsbergs sjukhus
Tegnérlunden
Strindbergsmuseet
Adolf Fredriks kyrka
Johannes kyrka
St Johannes Kyrkogård
Zita
Bonniers Konsthall
Drottningholm Slott
Barnhusviken
Sankt Eriksbron
Hötorget
NORRMALM
200 m
0.1 miles

★ TOP EXPERIENCE

Hagaparken

Part of the Royal National City Park, **Hagaparken** stretches from Vasastan to the neighbouring towns of Solna and Ulriksdal. This large green area is one of the most scenic places in Stockholm to walk, read or indulge in outdoor activities like boating and swimming.

An English Garden

Hagaparken is an enormous breath of fresh air in contrast to the industrial parks and highways nearby. The park is the best example of the English garden style, with manicured lawns and artificial water features.

Royal Quirks

If you enter through Vasastan you'll quickly encounter the lake, and then it's a bit of a walk to the north for the architectural follies that appealed to King Gustav III. There's the Chinese Temple, the Turkish Kiosk and the circus-like Koppartälten, which consists of three metal tents, one of which is now a cafe.

Gustav III's Paviljong (open May to September, though closed for renovations at the time of writing) is a superb example of neoclassical style; the furnishings and decor reflect King Gustav III's interest in all things Roman following his Italian tour in 1782.

Meanwhile, the steamy Fjärilshuset (Butterfly House) is ideal for a cold-weather visit. It has temperate and tropical rainforest sections; free-flying butterflies; turtles and tortoises; as well as tropical-fish tanks and a large shark aquarium.

MAP P130 **B1**

PLANNING TIP
Stockholm Odenplan tunnelbana station is close to the centre of Vasastan, and about a 10-minute walk from Hagaparken's south entrance.

Scan this QR code to download the free Kungliga Hovstaterna (Royal Walks) app for a guided tour.

★ TOP EXPERIENCE

Drottningholm Palace

Just 13km outside Stockholm is one of the most iconic palaces in Sweden's already impressive slate. **Drottningholm Slott** (Drottningholm Palace) is often referred to as Sweden's Versailles for its elaborate interiors and lush and expansive gardens. If you can spare the half-day trip, do it.

MAP P131 **A4**

PLANNING TIP
The palace closes at 4pm and the visit to the interiors takes at least an hour. If you arrive a little after 3pm you can still enter, but not after 3.30pm.

Scan this QR code to learn about summer boat trips to the palace.

Royal Opulence

The only word that can capture this immense castle and its impressive grounds is 'lush'. From the detailed interiors to the perfectly manicured gardens, Drottningholm Slott is the kind of place that comes to mind when palaces are mentioned. The UNESCO World Heritage–listed site and park was designed by Nicodemus Tessin the Elder and its construction began in 1662. By the time it was finished, it was a proof that the Swedish royals were ready to take up their place in European power politics. Take the one-hour guided tour of the palace, which provides more insight into the cultural milieu that influenced some of the sumptuous decorations, or download an audio guide in advance. Highlights include the maximalist State Bedchamber, Sweden's most expensive baroque interior; and the eye-boggling staircase, with statues and trompe l'oeil embellishments at every turn.

It's All in the Details

The palace has numerous fascinating outbuildings that are worth making time for. At the far end of the park is **Kina Slott** (May-Sep), a lavishly decorated Chinese pavilion built by King Adolf Fredrik as a birthday surprise for Queen Lovisa Ulrika in 1753. It has one of the finest rococo chinoiserie interiors in Europe. Also, don't miss the still-working Slottsteater, completed in 1766; it's the oldest theatre in the world

SUCHAN/SHUTTERSTOCK ©

still in its original state. The fascinating guided tour includes an Italianate room with fake 3D wall effects and a ceiling that looks like the sky. The Royal Chapel that was completed in 1730 is still used by Swedish royals today and staff of the royal court.

Out in the Garden

You could come to Drottningholm just for the grounds and still be immensely satisfied. From the main landing you can gaze out at the gardens, their geometrical design angled to impress. But the Hercules fountain, topiary and parterres are better explored in person, seemingly rolling into the distance infinitely in all directions. There are helpful signs throughout the park explaining the details that go into making a garden like this. The grounds are open to the public and you can picnic in Drottningholm park or grab lunch at Karamellan, beside the palace and with lake views from its outdoor seating.

WALKING TOUR

Vasastan

Vasastan is a residential and office district whose gems require a short history lesson and a little imagination to understand completely. It is a very pleasant neighbourhood to walk through with its wide pavements and plentiful small parks, not to mention the shaded bliss of Hagaparken nearby.

START	END	LENGTH
Stockholm Odenplan	Brunkeberg Tunnel	4km; one to two hours

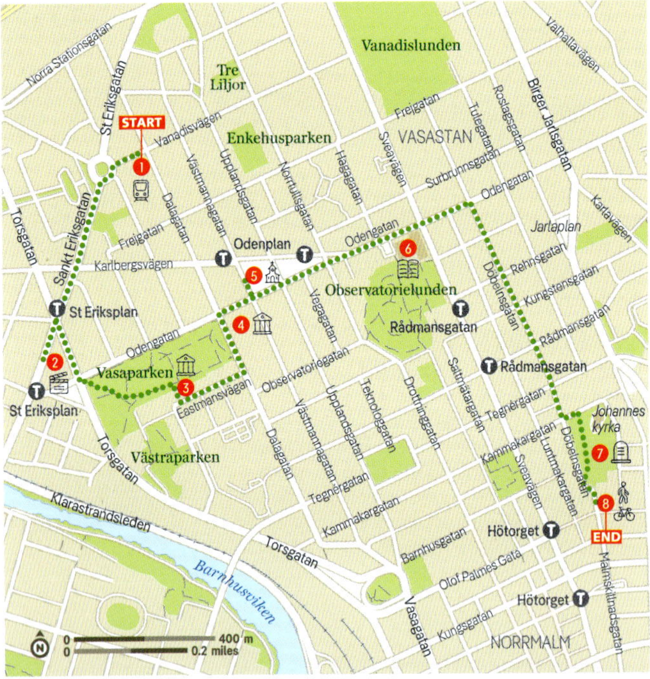

1 Stockholm Odenplan

Begin your walk at **Stockholm Odenplan** overground station (not Odenplan tunnelbana), one of the three largest stations in the city and an excellent place to catch connections to other parts of the city and outlying suburbs.

2 Bio Capitol Cinema

The **Bio Capitol** (p137) on Sant Eriksgatan is a 1926 art deco building that is a tribute to Sweden's rich filmmaking history. Carefully restored in 2018, this cinema is one of the most luxurious filmgoing experiences you'll ever have. There's a restaurant on-site too.

3 Sven-Harry's Konstmuseum

Around the corner inside the Vasaparken is **Sven-Harrys Konstmuseum** (p137), a modern art gallery celebrating the vast art collection of one of Sweden's leading architects alongside some rotating shows.

4 Astrid Lindgren's Hem

Children from around the world have found tremendous joy in Pippi Longstocking and other characters created by Astrid Lindgren, and the **Astrid Lindgren's Hem** museum (p136) in her former home on Dalagatan is where the magic of writing them happened.

5 Gustav Vasa Kyrka

At the heart of Stockholm on Odenplan plaza is one of the largest churches in Stockholm, the neo-baroque **Gustav Vasa Kyrka** (p139) with an impressive cupola.

6 Stadsbibliotek

One of the most impressive examples of the Swedish National Romantic style is the **Stadsbibliotek** (Stockholm City Library). It was closed for renovations at the time of writing.

7 St Johannes Kyrkogård

The area that is today known as **St Johannes Kyrkogård** (p139) on Dobëlnsgatan has been a burial ground for centuries and yet still attracts students from nearby schools as a park and playground. Wander around the cemetery in search of some of the oldest headstones.

8 Brunkeberg Tunnel

The 231m **Brunkeberg Tunnel** is used by cyclists and pedestrians to get around the traffic in the city centre. Although it was inaugurated in 1886, it has become one of the most popular spots to capture photos in the city.

EXPERIENCES

An Author's Sanctuary

MUSEUM

MAP: 1 P130 C3

With her red hair in crooked pigtails and a smattering of freckles across her nose, Pippi Longstocking is probably one of the most famous Swedes. Created by Astrid Lindgren to entertain her young daughter, the character draws visitors from all over the world looking to reconnect with their youth or pass on some of the magic to their children. Today, the flat where this acclaimed author lived and worked from 1941 up until her death in 2002 is a small museum: **Astrid Lindgren's Hem** *(astridlindgrenshem.se; 200kr)*. This is one of those places that's difficult to appreciate if you haven't read the books or are not familiar with just how big Pippi Longstocking was in her heyday. No Swedish author has been translated into as many languages as Astrid Lindgren. Tours are organised on specific dates, which are released at the beginning of every month on the Astrid Lindgren's Society website *(astridlindgrensallskapet.se)*.

An Icon at Home

MUSEUM

MAP: 2 P130 D4

Writer and painter August Strindberg (1849–1912) is considered the father of modern Swedish literature. For the final four years of his life, he lived in a small apartment in a building called the Blue Tower. Today the rooms are maintained as the evocative **Strindbergsmuseet** *(strindbergsmuseet.se; adult/student/child 100kr/75kr/free)*. Two groups of people would appreciate this museum: fans of Strindberg, and fans of historical furniture and decoration. Almost all of the early-20th-century furnishings and fixtures on display are the original ones, painstakingly collected and restored. Peep into his closet, scan his study and library (containing some 3000 volumes), do a round of the dining room and take in the often-absorbing temporary exhibits.

Artistic Time Capsule

MUSEUM

MAP: 3 P130 E1

One of Sweden's most celebrated 20th-century sculptors has left his mark all across city, including at the Stadshuset in Kungsholmen, and, in return, the home where he developed most of his ideas has been perfectly preserved as a museum. **The Carl Eldhs Ateljémuseum** *(eldhsatelje.se; adult/student/under-15s 120kr/100kr/free; Apr-Oct)* is a beautiful wooden building and garden next to Bellevue park that probably doesn't draw as many visitors as it should. The main attraction here is that the house and its contents have been left almost exactly as they were during Eldh's 30-year tenure. The space is also used for salons and intimate music and poetry performances. There's no cafe on-site – they're working on it – but it's small enough that you should have plenty of time to grab something to eat nearby.

A Day at the Cinema CINEMA

Completed in 1926, the Capitol was Vasastan's largest and finest cinema. The old version shut in 1985, but thanks to a successful Kickstarter campaign, the filmhouse has recently been reborn as the swanky **Bio Capitol** (MAP: 4 P131 **B3**, *capitolbio.se*), which you'll find screening indie, arthouse and retrospective films. There are four super-comfy auditoria in this art deco-styled space and they make cinema-going fun again with special events, such as screenings with afternoon tea served at your seat.

Around the corner on Odengatan is another retro charmer: **Konditori Ritorno** (MAP: 5 P131 **C3**, *ritorno.se*). This confectioner and cafe dating to 1959 is a hit with writers, students and pensioners, its worn leather chairs, chandeliers and old paintings making it a perfect pit stop for a coffee and heavenly *semla* (wheat-flour buns crammed with whipped cream and almond paste).

Arthouse Cinema CINEMA

MAP: 6 P130 **F4**

The oldest still-operational cinema in Stockholm, the **Zita** (*zita.se*) first opened its doors to the public in 1913, and while it has lived many lives under many names, it still plods on at Birger Jarlsgatan 37. Sure, you could just go there for a matinee – all films are screened in their original language – but it's much better when you know that this was at the heart of Sweden's 20th-century filmmaking history. Unlike other cinemas, much of the original decor and detail has been lost and it's less of an architectural draw, but if you love cinema and you have some downtime, swing by and enjoy being part of its long illustrious history – they have regular screenings of Swedish classics.

Billionaire's Delight MUSEUM

MAP: 7 P130 **C3**

The golden brass facade of the **Sven-Harrys Konstmuseum** (*sven-harrys.se; adult/student/under-18s; 220kr/190kr/free*) gleams on the south side of Vasaparken

SWEDISH ARCHITECTURAL STYLES

Have you ever looked at a building or a piece of furniture and known it was different from all the other ones around it but you couldn't explain why? A quick cheat code is that Swedish Grace refers to a style that mixes neoclassicism with local styles, for example at the Stadsbibliotek (p135), so look for columns and angles rather than the usual soft curves. Functionalism – as seen in much of the housing in Stockholm – is modernism that is a little less austere than brutalism, and of course, there are all the beautiful experimental works that defy categorisation.

making it a little hard to ignore – it's made of the same material that coats the euro. The building serves multiple functions. It stages interesting temporary exhibitions on a variety of themes, but the main attractions are its rooftop terrace and sculpture garden, surrounding a replica of rooms from Sven-Harry's former home: an 18th-century manor house on Lidingö, decorated with his extensive art and modern furniture collection. Pieces on display include works by August Strindberg, Gösta Adrian-Nilsson (GAN) and Carl Fredrick Hill. Access to these rooms is by guided tour (in Swedish). On the ground floor is **Guld**, a stylish cafe-bistro with terrace seating facing the park.

A Walk in the Park

PARK

MAP: 8 P130 B3

Vasaparken, a popular local park running alongside Odengatan, has something for everyone. The manicured lawns have won awards for how well they are laid out and maintained, and it's bursting with people in the summer enjoying an ice cream or a picnic. But the list of attractions goes on and on – there's a running track, football pitches (which transform into an ice rink in winter), a mini-golf putting course, a hilltop yoga pavilion, quieter spots to sit and read, and a giant playground where kids can run wild.

Art on the Tracks

MUSEUM

MAP: 9 P130 B4

Close to the train tracks and Vasaparken is one of Stockholm's newest and already iconic contemporary art galleries, the **Bonniers Konsthall** (*bonnierskonsthall.se; adult/student/under-26s 120kr/100kr/free; 11am-2pm Wed-Fri*), that celebrates contemporary art from Sweden and beyond. It's a very spare building with lots of natural light that is the perfect setting for the challenge of contemporary art that pushes boundaries and invites critical engagement. The gallery also sponsors prizes for up-and-coming artists, so it's a great place for collectors – real and dreamers – to

MOVIE MAGIC

There's a good chance that the most popular actor from mainland Europe that you know is Swedish, and that is because Sweden has always been a big cinema nation, dating all the way back to the silent era. Many of the world's best-known actors and directors from various eras are from Sweden, including Greta Garbo, Ingrid Bergman, filmmaker Ingmar Bergman, and the expansive Skarsgård clan. Relics from these icons are scattered around Stockholm, including a high concentration of the cinemas in the country that have witnessed and survived all of these eras in Vasastan.

CHURCH OF SWEDEN

The Church of Sweden is a Protestant and evangelical community that is part of the Lutheran family. In 1523 Gustav Vasa separated from the Catholic Church in part because the church in Rome refused to remove a bishop who had opposed the king during the Stockholm Bloodbath. The Church of Sweden was the official state church for several centuries, and this unique history plays out in the architecture of Swedish churches, which are more austere than those of their continental counterparts, but still retain a lot of flamboyant elements such as the imposing altarpiece at Gustav Vasa Kyrka.

identify the new voices emerging on the scene. Opening hours are limited, so if you're hoping to visit, plan accordingly.

Let Us Gather CHURCH

MAP: 10 P 130 **C2**

One of the oldest churches in Stockholm is the **Gustav Vasa Kyrka**, an architectural icon that is also at the heart of social programmes in the Vasastan area. The most notable detail in the church is the columbarium – a room where the ashes of the deceased are stored – one of the largest in Europe, speaking to the popularity of the practice in Sweden. The altarpiece that depicts the fall of Adam and Eve is the largest sculpture of its style in Sweden, while the distinct cupola rises over the nearby buildings making the church appear much larger than it is. The church also hosts lunchtime classical music concerts every Thursday and organ performances every Sunday, alongside art exhibitions from local artists. The church closes its doors at 6pm Monday to Thursday, and 3pm on Fridays so plan a visit earlier in the day, although it shouldn't take more than half an hour to experience most of the church.

Fun...at the Cemetery? CEMETERY

MAP: 11 P 130 **F4**

Some people like to hang out at **St Johannes Kyrkogård** (St John's Cemetery) even though it has been a burial site since at least the 13th century. This may just be a consequence of its location or because of the eerie calm that comes from it being a final resting place. St. John's Church on the grounds is also an interesting example of Swedish religious architecture, with the striped red-and-black brickwork extending to the interior, and there's a 17th-century clocktower on the grounds as well. If you're not too intimidated by the possibility of running into a ghost, you could join the ghost walks held here annually at the end of August. The church building is only open between 11am and 4pm.

LISTINGS

Best Places for...

See p131 for map of locations

€ Budget €€ Midrange €€€ Top End

Eating

Swedish Classics

Rolfs Kök €€€
12 E4
Delicious renditions of Swedish classics, including crispy potato pancakes with vendace roe, and red-wine-braised ox cheeks. *rolfskok.se; 11.30am-midnight Mon-Thu, to 1am Fri, 5pm-midnight Sat & Sun*

Tennstopet €€
13 C3
Stuffed deer heads and gilded mirrors at a traditional pub and restaurant serving fine Swedish classics. *tennstopet.se; 11.30am-midnight Mon-Fri, noon-1am Sat, noon-11pm Sun*

International Flavours

Babette €€
14 E2
A white-neon rooster welcomes you to this boisterous bistro where a tiny open kitchen pumps out pizzas with satisfying crispiness and delicious toppings. *babette.se, 5pm-1am*

Lao Wai €€
15 E3
Everything at this simple Chinese restaurant is gluten-free, vegan and sublime. *laowai.se; 5-10pm Mon-Sat*

Take Ramen €€
16 B3
Japanese-noodle heaven serving authentic bowls of steaming ramen. The vegetarian version is packed with flavour. *takeramen.com; 11am-9pm Mon-Fri, from noon Sat & Sun*

Fika & Sandwiches

Cafe Pascal €
17 D2
Sip your coffee and tuck into a sandwich at this hipster cafe that doubles as a gallery. *cafepascal.se; 7am-7pm Mon-Fri, 8am-5pm Sat & Sun*

Lillebrors Bageri €
18 A3
Fresh bakes in front of a street that goes car-free in the summer. *lillebrors.se; 8am-7pm Mon-Fri, to 5pm Sat & Sun*

ANALIA GLOGOWSKI/LONELY PLANET ©

Drinking

After-Work Hangouts

Le Bon Plat
19 B3
French bistro and wine bar that's great for drinks, aperitifs and occasionally a pavement DJ.
lebonplat.se; 4-9pm Mon, noon-10pm Tue-Sat

Bara Caisas
20 C3
Swedish food and drink in a cosy atmosphere.
4-10pm Tue-Fri, from 1pm Sat & Sun

Shopping

Second-Hand

Arkivet Second Hand
21 C2
Second-hand store designed to showcase the clothes rather than overwhelm the browser.
arkivet.com; 11am-6pm Mon-Fri, to 5pm Sat, noon-4pm Sun

Worn Vintage
22 B2
High-end second-hand leather and outerwear that is a favourite with celebs. Second-hand doesn't mean cheap.
wornvintage.se; 10am-5pm Thu & by appointment

SOLARBOATS
BOAT!

Stockholm Toolkit

View of Strandvägen, Östermalm (p101)

TRABANTOS/SHUTTERSTOCK ©

Family Travel

Stockholm is one of the most child-friendly cities in Europe, if not the world, with many places curating special activities and opportunities for children. High accessibility also means it's easier to navigate with buggies and prams.

Trading Places

While the city itself is quite child-friendly, some of the attractions might be quite boring for younger kids. One way you could navigate this is to trade one grown-up attraction for one kids' attraction so everyone gets some fun.

EATING OUT

Children are generally welcome in restaurants and even pubs, but not bars, with many places offering children's menus that feature smaller portions for slightly less. Ask the waiters before you order.

Children Go Free!

Almost all museums in Stockholm are free for children, but the exact age cut-off varies between 12 and 26! Plenty of museums also offer audio guides specifically for children, as well as activities that will help them navigate the museum semi-independently. Always ask what your young traveller is eligible for at the front desk or consult the website before your visit.

Breastfeeding in Stockholm

Breastfeeding in public is widely acceptable in Stockholm and barely noticed. Some places offer lactating pods or rooms, particularly in shopping malls.

Public Transport

Up to six children under 11 can travel free with one adult.

Playgrounds in Stockholm

There are parks with playgrounds in every neighbourhood in Stockholm. Some of the best include Humlegårdens Parklek in Östermalm, Ivar Los park in Södermalm and Rålambshovsparken in Kungsholmen.

Accommodation

Each of Stockholm's districts has a distinct vibe and you might want to stay close to things you enjoy.

Where to stay if you love...

Open spaces and walks along the water

Kungsholmen (p115) Has some amazing parks and sunset views, particularly in Rålambshovparken and Smedsuddsbadet, and it's also close to Långholmen.

Late nights with affordable drinks

Södermalm (p99) Stockholm's hub for fun and an affordable night out. Hornsgatan, the main street, is a lightning rod for after-work drinks.

OUR PICK

We love to stay in...

Södermalm (p87) This is the perfect balance of being in the centre of things without being overwhelmed, with excellent transport connections to everywhere else if you need them, and plentiful high-end and value budget options. Visit the SoFo neighbourhood for food and shopping at any price point.

HOW MUCH FOR A NIGHT IN

A hostel **230kr**

A mid-range chain hotel **950kr**

A central hotel **1400kr**

High-end shopping and dining

Östermalm (p112) Celebs love Östermalm, and so will you if your holiday is incomplete without a quick stop at a designer store. Try Sturegallerian for a taste of high-end shopping.

Museums and history

Norrmalm (p58) An impressive selection of museums, it's also within walking distance of Gamla Stan and Djurgården. Plus it has the best selection of budget hotels.

To be away from the crowds

Vasastan (p61) Primarily residential district that offers a bit more quiet in a pretty quiet town. You'll be 10 minutes away from Hagaparken and a small urban hike.

Food, Drink & Nightlife

Allergies & Intolerances

Staff in restaurants in Stockholm are very sensitive to diners with intolerances and allergies, and the allergens that may be present in food are usually indicated on the menu. Servers will also usually ask you if you have any allergies when you ask for recommendations.

HOW TO SAY

I am allergic to... Jag är allergisk mot...
nuts nötter
shellfish skaldjur
dairy mejeriprodukter
gluten gluten

HOW TO ASK...

Is this gluten free?
Är detta/denna glutenfritt?
Does this contain nuts?
Innehåller detta nötter?
Is there a vegan option?
Finns det ett veganskt alternativ?

GO MEATLESS

Vegans and vegetarians will never lack options in Stockholm, with most restaurants serving at least one option for each and several restaurants in all the districts dedicated to both. Sustainable restaurants specialising in seasonal and local produce are also the rage at every price point.

Fika

A *fika* is just a coffee and a pastry, but it is integral to Swedish social life. *Fika* often refers to the act of grabbing a coffee rather than the drink itself, and an invitation to grab a *fika* is more about the company than the meal.

HOW TO... Pay the Bill

English is everywhere but you could get the server's attention with '*ursäkta mij*' which means 'excuse me', and say '*täck*' for 'thank you' or 'if you please'.

Bills: It's rare to settle bills in cash; card payments are expected. Bills are generally split equally.

Tipping: This is not generally expected but, with the influx of tourists, you might be presented with a card machine that invites you to tip a preset amount. You can skip this as a service charge for staff is included in the bill. If you do want to tip, 5–10% is acceptable, and up to 15% for exceptional service.

PRICE RANGES

€
less than €150

€€
€150–400

€€€
more than €400

OPENING HOURS

Cafes 7.30am to 6pm
Restaurants: 11am- 3pm; dinner: 5pm-10pm (many restaurants serve all day)
Fast-food joints 11am-late

Going Out

Bar scene Nights out in Stockholm can either involve bars where talking descends into dancing, or club nights. For the former, dressing up a little is advised – think nice jeans with a cute pair of flats. **Lilla Baren at Riche** (p113) and **Stjärtilleriet** (p113) in Östermalm are popular with local celebrities.

Rave culture Stockholm, is home to one of the biggest techno scenes in the world. Dress codes are a little more casual here but you're still expected to make a bit of an effort. **Huset under Bron** (p94) in Södermalm is an excellent introduction to the scene.

Live music Seeing a live act is also a great night out in Stockholm. **Fasching** (p58) is a staple. Plan to arrive at around 11pm for a big night out, with closing hours varying from 2am to 3am with a hard stop. Age limits are strictly enforced at 20 to 23 years old.

HOW MUCH FOR A

Pint of beer
100kr

Glass of wine
30–50kr

Cocktail in an upscale bar
170kr

Bottle of beer from a Systembolaget (state-owned liquor store) 20kr

Coffee
35kr

Kebab platter
180kr

Cinnamon pastry (*kanelbullar*)
25kr

LGBTIQ+ Travellers

Stockholm is one of the most LGBTIQ-friendly cities with almost all spaces declaring themselves friendly.

Gaybourhoods

Stockholm has a long history of being LGBTIQ-friendly, including within religious institutions like churches. There are no true 'gaybourhoods' because people have never felt the need to converge for safety. There are a handful of gay clubs and bars that specifically cater to LGBTIQ+ communities – try **Lucy's Flower Shop** in Östermalm and **Mälarpaviljongen** in Kungsholmen, which only opens in the summer.

Even so, the risk for spontaneous violence still exists, particularly after a night out. In general people in Stockholm are less likely to indulge in public displays of affection and, for LGBTIQ+ people, the risk of being threatened for PDA is, unfortunately, still present. Drag performances do happen but not as frequently as in larger cities. Try **The Blue Oyster** to the west of Södermalm.

OUR PICKS

Stockholm Pride

Stockholm Pride is the largest pride festival in Europe. More than a parade, the events spread out over the entire last week of July into early August, involving parties and music performances, but also talks and speeches. As an organisation, Stockholm Pride also raises money for solidarity with LGBTIQ+ organisations throughout Sweden and beyond, so it's a great opportunity to give back.

ACOMMODATION DURING PRIDE

It's more affordable to stay in outlying districts like Solna that are well-served by public transport during Pride weekend.

REGULAR QUEER-FRIENDLY EVENTS

The Blue Oyster is one of the best-known LGBTIQ+ bars in Stockholm and hosts regular events.

Resources

● **RFSL** (rfsl.se) The Swedish Federation for Lesbian, Gay, Bisexual, Transgender, Queer and Intersex Rights offers support, including legal advocacy. ● **Stockholm Pride** (stockholmpride.org) More than a party, it also hosts events throughout the year.

Health & Safe Travel

Stockholm is generally safe to visit, although caution is always advisable.

TAP WATER

The tap water in Stockholm is perfectly safe to drink and you can expect to be offered tap water in restaurants unless you explicitly ask for bottled water. There are water fountains in parks for both people and their four-legged friends.

Health in a Hurry

If you fall ill, dial 1177 to speak to a nurse who can offer options to treat your condition yourself or direct you to more resources. Calls are charged at a standard rate and the advice is free. EU and UK citizens with an EHIC card are treated as citizens (free), while non-EU/EEA citizens need to either provide proof of insurance from their home country or comprehensive health insurance, or pay out of pocket.

Legal Age

The legal drinking age in Sweden is 18, but some bars will raise it to 20 or 23.

Buying Medicine in Stockholm

Some over-the-counter medications like painkillers and cough medicine can be bought directly from the pharmacy or even at a petrol station. Prescription medicines can only be purchased with a current prescription from a pharmacy. Prescriptions are free for people with a residence permit up to a threshold, but others must pay full price.

E-SCOOTERS

You can rent an e-scooter in Stockholm but under-15s must wear a helmet and you must only leave it in designated areas.

QUICK INFO

Cannabis

Cannabis is illegal to posses and consume, and penalties are stiff.

Security

Lock up bicycles – bike theft is one of the most common crimes in Stockholm.

Public drinks

Drinking at night in some parks may be prohibited – check signage.

Responsible Travel

Follow these tips to leave a lighter footprint, support local and have a positive impact on communities.

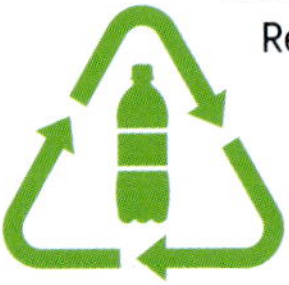

Read the Label!

Returnpak or Pantamera is the bottle-deposit-and-return system in Sweden. A small deposit of 1-2kr is added to the price of tinned and bottled goods manufactured in Sweden (including PET bottles), and you can get this back if you return the disused container to widely available machines in large grocery stores and even some bars and clubs.

Go with Others

There's no reason for a rental car if you're exclusively in Stockholm and the archipelago. Invest in the SL travel card instead and use the public transport system.

OUR PICK

Sustainability
Rosendals Trädgårdskafe (p84) is more than a restaurant, selling craft goods made on-site, and offering courses on gardening and flower-picking in season.

Bike Rental

Sweden's bike-share programme is currently being revamped but there are several private rental options on the various islands. In Gamla Stan, Gamla Stans Cykel (p47) offers bike rentals and tours throughout the old town. In Djurgården, bikes and bike tours are available at the Royal Djurgården Visitor Center (p77) and Rent a Bike in Strandvägen. Weelo (weelo.tours) offers e-bike rentals and curated tours.

Resources

- **activescandinavia.com** Active Scandinavia offers self-guided bike tours across Stockholm and beyond.
- **visitstockholm.com/see-do/attractions/have-a-sustainable-stay-in-stockholm** Pick from one of Stockholm's sustainable hotels.

FROM LEFT: JOMIC/SHUTTERSTOCK ©, MANU PADILLA/SHUTTERSTOCK ©

DRINKS WITHOUT MILES

Brännerian Bar (p99) in Södermalm works to reduce its carbon footprint by producing all its drinks and spirits on-site and substituting ingredients in their cocktails with local alternatives.

Second-Hand Shopping

Second-hand shopping at various price points is very popular in Stockholm and this is a great place to find timeless classics. Judits (p99) is a favourite for clothing. Arkivet Second Hand (p141) curates its offering so that they are second-hand but on trend. Worn Vintage (p141) in Vasastan offers high-end vintage clothing and is very popular with local and international celebrities. Humana (p99) and the Stockholm Stadsmission (p127) offer second-hand shopping with a social conscience as proceeds go towards supporting various social programmes.

SUSTAINABLE EATING

The restaurant at Fotografiska (p90) in Södermalm has received two of the highest international awards available for sustainability. Pricey but it's worth it.

Climate Change & Travel

It's impossible to ignore the impact we have when travelling. Lonely Planet urges all travellers to engage with their travel carbon footprint, which will mainly come from air travel. While there often isn't an alternative, travellers can look to minimise the number of flights they take, opt for newer aircrafts and use cleaner ground transport, such as trains. One proposed solution – purchasing carbon offsets – unfortunately does not cancel out the impact of individual flights. While most destinations will depend on air travel for the foreseeable future, for now, pursuing ground-based travel where possible is the best course of action.

The **UN Carbon Offset Calculator** shows how flying impacts a household's emissions

The **ICAO's carbon emissions calculator** allows visitors to analyse the CO^2 generated by point-to-point journeys

Accessible Travel

Public Transport

All forms of public transport in Stockholm are generally easily accessible. The SL company that manages public transport in the city also offers a sustainability guarantee, so if you are unable to reach your destination using public transport, they will offer support. Call +20 120 20 22 or send a text message to +70 256 46 81.

Older Travellers

Concessions on entry fees are available at various sites across Stockholm for senior citizens, even if they do not require specific support to access the venue. Some museums also offer wheelchairs and hearing loops where needed – always ask.

The Mobility Service

If your trip cannot be completed using public transport, book an accessible trip up to 28 days in advance by calling +08-720 80 00 or visiting fardtjansten.regionstockholm.se.

ACCESSIBLE TOURS

There are companies that specialise in offering accessible tours across Stockholm. Try Stockholm by Sophie (sophieheine.se).

OUR PICK

The **Nationalmuseum** (p61) is probably the most accessible museum in a city where accessibility is a major priority. Aside from ramps and handrails, a lift offers access from the street and there is a tactile map in the lobby for visually impaired visitors. They also loan out magnifying glasses and wheeled walking frames or wheelchairs for those who need it, and there are accessible toilets on every floor. Admission is free for accompanying persons.

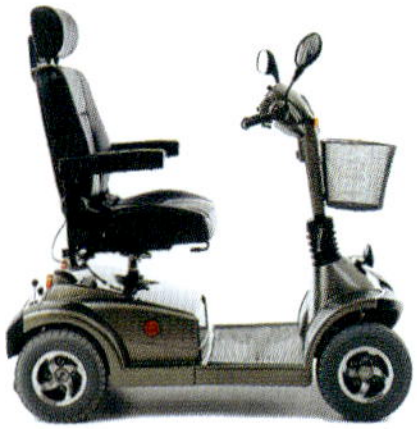

NAVIGATING GAMLA STAN

Most of the streets in Gamla Stan are cobblestoned, presenting particular difficulty for those travelling in wheelchairs. A motorised wheelchair or a golf-cart tour (p47) is recommended.

Resources

- **t-d.se/en** The Accessibility Database allows you to research the accessibility of thousands of hotels and venues in Sweden before you arrive.

Nuts & Bolts

Opening Hours

Expect seasonal changes with shorter hours in the winter. Check ahead.

Banks 10am-3pm

Bars 7pm-midnight

Cafes 7am-7pm

Clubs 5pm-3am

Post Offices Hours vary. Pay for postage online (postnord.se/en/private/sending) and drop off at various locations.

Restaurants 10am-11pm (some close for breaks during the day)

Shops 9am-6pm (many close earlier on Saturday and remain closed on Sunday)

Supermarkets 6am-7pm

ELECTRICITY

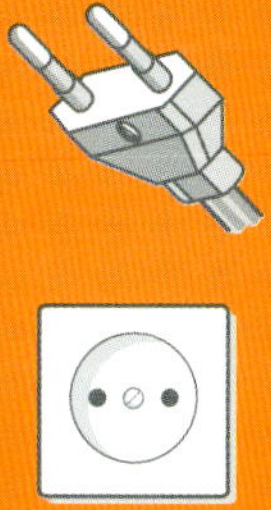

Type C
220V/50Hz

Type F
230V/50Hz

Öppen
Open
Stängd
Closed

Public Holidays

Midsummer brings life almost to a halt for three days from the preceding Thursday: transport and services are reduced, and shops and tourist offices close, as do some attractions.

New Year's Day 1 January

Epiphany 6 January

Good Friday/Easter Sunday/Easter Monday March/April

May Day 1 May

Ascension Day May/June

National Day 6 June

Whit Sunday Late May/early June

Midsummer's Day Third Friday in June

All Saints' Day 1 November

Christmas Day 25 December

Boxing Day 26 December

QUICK INFO

Time Zone Central European Time (GMT/UTC+1 in winter, +2 during daylight savings)

Country Code +46

Emergency Number 112

Population 1.7 million

NO SMOKING

Smoking is frowned upon in Sweden as a result of heavy campaigning and also the popularity of smoke-free alternatives, such as *snus* (chewing tobacco). It's banned in bus terminals and restaurants (inside and out), as well as parks and any enclosed sporting venues.

Language

Swedish Basics

Hello.
Hej. *hey*

Goodbye.
Hej då./Adjö. *hey daw/aa·yeu*

Yes.
Ja. *yaa*

No.
Nej. *ney*

Please.
Tack. *tak*

Thank you (very much).
Tack (så mycket). *tak (saw mew·ke)*

You're welcome.
Varsågod. var·sha·gohd

Excuse me.
Ursäkta mig. *oor·shek·ta mey*

Sorry.
Förlåt. *feur·lawt*

Fast Phrases

How are you?
Hur mår du? *hoor mawr doo*

Fine, thanks. And you?
Bra, tack. Och dig? *braa tak o dey*

What's your name?
Vad heter du? *vaad hey·ter doo*

My name is ...
Jag heter ... *yaa hey·ter ...*

Do you speak English?
Talar du engelska? *taa·lar doo eng·el·ska*

I don't understand.
Jag förstår inte. *yaa feur·shtawr in·te*

Where's the ...?
Var ligger ...? *var li·ger ...*

What's the address?
Vilken adress är det? *vil·ken a·dres air de*

Can you show me (on the map)?
Kan du visa mig (på kartan)?
kan doo vee·sa mey? (paw kar·tan)

How far is it?
Hur långt är det? *hoor lawngt air de*

How do I get there?
Hur kommer man dit?
hoor ko·mar man deet

Numbers

1 **ett** *et*

2 **två** *tvaw*

3 **tre** *trey*

4 **fyra** *few·ra*

5 **fem** *fem*

10 Phrases to Sound Like a Local

Cool! **Cool!** *kool*

No worries. **Inga problem.** *eng-aa proo-blem*

Sure. **Javisst.** *yuh-vist*

No way! **Det menar du inte?** *deh mea-narr du in-teh*

Just joking! **Jag skojar bara!** *yuh sko-yar ba-rah*

Too bad. **Vad synd.** *vuh sünd*

What a shame. **Vad tråkigt.** *vuh trro-kigt*

What's up? **Läget?** *lae-geht*

Well done! **Bra jobbat.** *brrah jo-bat*

Not bad. **Inte illa.** *en-teh e-lah*

THE SPOKEN WORD

The standard language or **rikssvenska** *(reeks·sven·ska; lit: kingdom-Swedish)* is based on dialects from around Stockholm. Some of the rural dialects are quite diverse, so don't be surprised to hear different words or pronunciations away from the capital.

The Written Word

The missionaries who introduced Christianity in the 12th century brought the Roman alphabet, but some modification was necessary to represent the specific vowel sounds, so additional letters were developed – represented as *å*, *ä* and *ö*. These come at the end of the Swedish alphabet.

DISTINCTIVE SOUNDS

Most Swedish sounds are similar to their English counterparts. One exception is fh – a breathy sound pronounced with rounded lips, like saying 'f' and 'w' at the same time.

WHO SPEAKS SWEDISH?

In neighbouring Finland, Swedish shares official status with Finnish and is a mandatory subject in schools, but it's the first language for only about 6% of the population. Norwegian and Danish are closely related to Swedish, and speakers of the three languages are often able to communicate with one another in their own tongues. PS: Any traveller to Sweden should know that the Swedish Chef from the Muppets doesn't really speak Swedish at all.

6	7	8	9	10
sex *seks*	**sju** *fhoo*	**åtta** *o·ta*	**nio** *nee·oh*	**tio** *tee·oh*

Index

Sights p000 Map pages **p000**

See also separate subindexes for:
Eating p156
Drinking p156
Shopping p156

Eating

Drinking

Shopping

Send Us Your Feedback

We love to hear from travellers – your comments help make our books better. We read every word, and we guarantee that your feedback goes straight to the authors. Visit lonelyplanet.com/contact to submit your updates and suggestions.

Note: We may edit, reproduce and incorporate your comments in Lonely Planet products such as guidebooks, websites and digital products, so let us know if you are happy to have your name acknowledged. For a copy of our privacy policy visit lonelyplanet.com/legal.

Acknowledgements

Cover photograph: Gamla Stan. Ken Scicluna/AWL Images ©

Back photograph: Drottningholm Palace Garden. Collection Maykova/ Shutterstock ©

THIS BOOK

Destination Editor
Amy Lynch

Cartographer
Julie Sheridan

Production Editor
Graham O'Neill

Book Designer
Carol Farrell

Assisting Editors
Sofie Andersen, Melanie Dankel

Cover Researcher
Kat Marsh

Thanks to
Ronan Abayawickrema

Published by Lonely Planet Global Limited
CRN 554153

6th edition – Jul 2025

ISBN 978 1 83758 369 0

10 9 8 7 6 5 4 3 2 1

Printed in Malaysia